Crochet Stories
Grimms' Fairy Tales

Vanessa Putt

Photography by
Gloria Cavallaro

Dover Publications, Inc.
Mineola, New York

Copyright

Copyright © 2016 by Vanessa Putt
All rights reserved.

Bibliographical Note

Crochet Stories: Grimms' Fairy Tales is a new work, first published by
Dover Publications, Inc., in 2016. The fairy tale story texts are taken
from standard editions.

International Standard Book Number

ISBN-13: 978-0-486-79461-7
ISBN-10: 0-486-79461-X

Manufactured in the United States by RR Donnelley
79461X01   2016
www.doverpublications.com

Contents

General Notes, Tips, and Abbreviations

Working in the Round

Most of the patterns in this book are worked in the round. A couple are worked in a continuous spiral, but most are worked in joined, separate rounds. Either way they are worked, you will want to use a removable stitch marker to mark the first stitch of every round to keep track of where you're beginning. Sl sts and ch 1 sts, to complete and start rounds/rows, do not count as sts and do not factor into st counts for the rounds or rows.

Stuffing

Polyfil stuffing is used for the projects in this book. Some pieces, such as the gingerbread house, the tower, and the beanstalk, will stand up better with some weight added to the bottom. When you stuff, add dried beans, rice, or pennies in the bottom of the piece, and then fill in the remainder with stuffing. *Caution:* Items with added weight, and/or small pieces, in the bottom are not suitable for children under 3 years old and should not be used.

Gauge and Measurements

Gauge is not critical when making amigurumi. Yarn recommendations and hook sizes are given, but the most important thing is to work the pieces tightly enough so that the fabric is solid and the stuffing doesn't show through. This is why a smaller hook is used than what would normally be used with the yarn.

Differences in the overall measurements can occur, depending on how tightly or loosely the crocheter works, as well as on which yarn is chosen. Even yarns within the same weight category can yield different gauges and measurements overall. *Super Saver Economy* ® by Red Heart® is slightly on the heavier side of worsted weight, and *Deborah Norville Collection Everyday®Soft Worsted Solids* by Premier® Yarns is slightly on the lighter side of worsted weight. This means that even though Jack and the Prince are both the same pattern and are both worked in worsted weight, the overall measurements are different.

Using a different weight of yarn is the easiest way to change the size of your characters. The Giant is worked in the same basic person pattern as the rest of the characters, but since he's worked in a super bulky yarn, he's much bigger than the rest. Alternately, the same pattern worked in a fingering weight yarn will create a mini version of the characters in this book.

Finishing

Details for Making Your Character Special

The differences are in the details! It's the little things, like embroidery, faces, and hair, that will make your characters unique. Instead of adhering exactly to the patterns in this book, try changing the shapes and colors of the details to make the characters yours.

Some items, such as safety eyes, have to be added before you stuff and finish the piece, but I prefer to do as much of the sewing and embroidery as possible *after* the piece is stuffed and finished. If you feel more comfortable adding details before finishing, it is possible to do this. It also can be easier to add the details after, as the shape of the piece can change between crocheting and stuffing. I find it much simpler to add the details after characters are as final as possible—that way it is very easy to judge where you're placing the details.

The instructions are written so that the arms are sewn on after the body is finished and stuffed, but this is something that would be very easy to do while you're still crocheting the body.

Faces

I used safety eyes for all of the pieces, but you can just as easily use black yarn or embroidery thread to sew on eyes. You can also find different colors of safety eyes, such as the brown eyes used in the Giant in "Jack and the Beanstalk."

I chose not to add facial features beyond the eyes, but you can embroider or paint full faces on your characters. You can also cut the features out of felt or fabric and stitch them on.

Weaving in Ends

As with the embroidery and sewn-on details, I prefer to weave in ends after the piece has been finished and stuffed. Weaving in your ends this way is very easy, and a great way to secure the ends into your piece. To do so, weave back and forth next to where the end is—then insert the yarn needle into your piece and out an opposite side, preferably on the back or underside of the piece. Cut the end close to the piece. Running the end through the stuffing will help to secure the yarn and prevent it from coming out.

Abbreviations

approx approximately

beg beginning

ch chain

cm centimeters

dc double crochet

dec('d) decrease(d)

foll following

hdc half double crochet

hdc2tog half double crochet 2 stitches together

inc increase

m meter(s)

mm millimeter(s)

oz ounce(s)

rem remain(s)(ing)

rep repeat

rnd round

RS right side

sc single crochet

sc2tog single crochet 2 stitches together

sk skip

sl slip

st(s) stitch(es)

tog together

tr treble crochet

WS wrong side

* repeat directions following *

[ ] repeat directions inside brackets

Basic Person Pattern

SKILL LEVEL
Easy

Things you'll need:

THE YARN

Super Saver Economy® by Red Heart®, 7oz/198g skeins, each approx 364yds/333m

* 1 skein in #313 Aran

Note This is what was used for this particular example, but you can use any worsted weight yarn, the same size hook, and any color for this pattern.

THE HOOK

Size G/6 (4mm) crochet hook

ADDITIONAL MATERIALS

Yarn needle
Polyfil stuffing
2 black safety eyes 6mm

MEASUREMENTS

Height 5¼" / 13.5cm

GAUGE

Gauge is not critical.

BASIC PERSON

Head

Ch 3, join with sl st to form ring.

Rnd 1: Ch 1, sc 6 into ring, sl st in beg ch.

Inc rnd 2: Ch 1, 2 sc in each st around, sl st in first sc of rnd—12 sc.

Inc rnd 3: Ch 1, *2 sc in first st, sc in next st; rep from * around, sl st in first st of rnd—18 sc.

Inc rnd 4: Ch 1, *2 sc in first st, sc in next 2 sts; rep from * around, sl st in first st of rnd—24 sc.

Inc rnd 5: Ch 1, *2 sc in first st, sc in next 3 sts; rep from * around, sl st in first st of rnd—30 sc.

Rnds 6–11: Ch 1, sc in each st around, sl st in first st of rnd.

Place safety eyes between rnds 7 and 8, 4 sc apart.

Dec rnd 12: Ch 1, *sc2tog, sc in next 3 sts; rep from * around, sl st in first st of rnd—24 sc.

Hansel and Gretel

Hansel and Gretel

Hard by a great forest dwelt a poor wood-cutter with his wife and his two children. The boy was called Hansel and the girl Gretel. He had little to bite and to break, and once when great dearth fell on the land, he could no longer procure even daily bread. Now when he thought over this by night in his bed, and tossed about in his anxiety, he groaned and said to his wife: "What is to become of us? How are we to feed our poor children, when we no longer have anything even for ourselves?" "I'll tell you what, husband," answered the woman, "early tomorrow morning we will take the children out into the forest to where it is the thickest; there we will light a fire for them, and give each of them one more piece of bread, and then we will go to our work and leave them alone. They will not find the way home again, and we shall be rid of them." "No, wife," said the man, "I will not do that; how can I bear to leave my children alone in the forest?—the wild animals would soon come and tear them to pieces." "O, you fool!" said she, "then we must all four die of hunger, you may as well plane the planks for our coffins," and she left him no peace until he consented. "But I feel very sorry for the poor children, all the same," said the man.

The two children had also not been able to sleep for hunger, and had heard what their stepmother had said to their father. Gretel wept bitter tears, and said to Hansel: "Now all is over with us." "Be quiet, Gretel," said Hansel, "do not distress yourself, I will soon find a way to help us." And when the old folks had fallen asleep, he got up, put on his little coat, opened the door below, and crept outside. The moon shone brightly, and the white pebbles which lay in front of the house glittered like real silver pennies. Hansel stooped and stuffed the little pocket of his coat with as many as he could get in. Then he went back and said to Gretel:

"Be comforted, dear little sister, and sleep in peace, God will not forsake us," and he lay down again in his bed. When day dawned, but before the sun had risen, the woman came and awoke the two children, saying: "Get up, you sluggards! We are going into the forest to fetch wood." She gave each a little piece of bread, and said: "There is something for your dinner, but do not eat it up before then, for you will get nothing else." Gretel took the bread under her apron, as Hansel had the pebbles in his pocket. Then they all set out together on the way to the forest. When they had walked a short time, Hansel stood still and peeped back at the house, and did so again and again. His father said: "Hansel, what are you looking at there and staying behind for? Pay attention, and do not forget how to use your legs." "Ah, father,' said Hansel, "I am looking at my little white cat, which is sitting up on the roof, and wants to say goodbye to me." The wife said: "Fool, that is not your little cat, that is the morning sun which is shining on the chimneys." Hansel, however, had not been looking back at the cat, but had been constantly throwing one of the white pebble-stones out of his pocket on the road.

When they had reached the middle of the forest, the father said: "Now, children, pile up some wood, and I will light a fire that you may not be cold." Hansel and Gretel gathered brushwood together, as high as a little hill. The brushwood was lighted, and when the flames were burning very high, the woman said: "Now, children, lay yourselves down by the fire and rest, we will go into the forest and cut some wood. When we have done, we will come back and fetch you away."

Hansel and Gretel sat by the fire, and when noon came, each ate a little piece of bread, and as they heard the strokes of the wood-axe they believed that their father was near. It was not the axe, however, but a branch which he had fastened to a withered tree which the wind was blowing backwards and forwards. And as they had been sitting such a long time, their eyes closed with fatigue, and they fell fast asleep. When at last they awoke, it was already dark night. Gretel began to cry and said: 'How are we to get out of the forest now?' But Hansel comforted her and said: "Just wait a little, until the moon has risen, and then we will soon find the way." And when the full moon had risen, Hansel took his little sister by the hand, and followed the pebbles which shone like newly-coined silver pieces, and showed them the way.

They walked the whole night long, and by break of day came once more to their father's house. They knocked at the door, and when the woman opened it and saw that it was Hansel and Gretel, she said: "You naughty children, why have you slept so long in the forest?—we thought you were never coming back at all!" The father, however, rejoiced, for it had cut him to the heart to leave them behind alone.

Not long afterwards, there was once more great dearth throughout the land, and the children heard their mother saying at night to their father: "Everything is eaten again, we have one half loaf left, and that is the end. The children must go, we will take them farther into the wood, so that they will not find their way out again; there is no other means of saving ourselves!" The man's heart was heavy, and he thought: "It would be better for you to share the last mouthful with your children." The woman, however, would listen to nothing that he had to say, but scolded and reproached him. He who says A must say B, likewise, and as he had yielded the first time, he had to do so a second time also.

The children, however, were still awake and had heard the conversation. When the old folks were asleep, Hansel again got up, and wanted to go out and pick up pebbles as he had done before, but the woman had locked the door, and Hansel could not get out. Nevertheless he comforted his little sister, and said: "Do not cry, Gretel, go to sleep quietly, the good God will help us."

Early in the morning came the woman, and took the children out of their beds. Their piece of bread was given to them, but it was still smaller than the time before. On the way into the forest Hansel crumbled his in his pocket, and often stood still and threw a morsel on the ground. "Hansel, why do you stop and look round?" said the father, "go on." "I am looking back at my little pigeon which is sitting on the roof, and wants to say goodbye to me," answered Hansel. "Fool!" said the woman, "that is not your little pigeon, that is the morning sun that is shining on the chimney." Hansel, however, little by little, threw all the crumbs on the path.

The woman led the children still deeper into the forest, where they had never in their lives been before. Then a great fire was again made, and the mother said: "Just sit there, you children, and when you are tired you may sleep a little; we are going into the forest to cut wood, and in the evening when we are done, we will come and fetch you away." When it was noon, Gretel shared her piece of bread with Hansel, who had scattered his by the way. Then they fell asleep and evening passed, but no one came to the poor children. They did not awake until it was dark night, and Hansel comforted his little sister and said: "Just wait, Gretel, until the moon rises, and then we shall see the crumbs of bread which I have strewn about, they will show us our way home again." When the moon came they set out, but they found no crumbs, for the many thousands of birds which fly about in the woods and fields had picked them all up. Hansel said to Gretel: "We shall soon find the way," but they did not find it. They walked the whole night and all the next day too from morning till evening, but they did not get out of the forest, and were very hungry, for they had nothing to eat but two or three berries, which grew on the ground. And as they were so weary that their legs would carry them no longer, they lay down beneath a tree and fell asleep.

It was now three mornings since they had left their father's house. They began to walk again, but they always came deeper into the forest, and if help did not come soon, they must die of hunger and weariness. When it was mid-day, they saw a beautiful snow-white bird sitting on a bough, which sang so delightfully that they stood still and listened to it. And when its song was over, it spread its wings and flew away before them, and they followed it until they reached a little house, on the roof of which it alighted; and when they approached the little house they saw that it was built of bread and covered with cakes, but that the windows were of clear sugar. "We will set to work on that," said Hansel, "and have a good meal. I will eat a bit of the roof, and you, Gretel, can eat some of the window, it will taste sweet." Hansel reached up above, and broke off a little of the roof to try how it tasted, and Gretel leant against the window and nibbled at the panes. Then a soft voice cried from the parlour:

"Nibble, nibble, gnaw,
Who is nibbling at my little house?"

The children answered:

"The wind, the wind,
The heaven-born wind,"

and went on eating without disturbing themselves. Hansel, who liked the taste of the roof, tore down a great piece of it, and Gretel pushed out the whole of one round window-pane, sat down, and enjoyed herself with it. Suddenly the door opened, and a woman as old as the hills, who supported herself on crutches, came creeping out. Hansel and Gretel were so terribly frightened that they let fall what they had in their hands. The old woman, however, nodded her head, and said: "Oh, you dear children, who has brought you here? Do come in, and stay with me. No harm shall happen to you." She took them both by the hand, and led them into her little house. Then good food was set before them, milk and pancakes, with sugar, apples, and nuts. Afterwards two pretty little beds were covered with clean white linen, and Hansel and Gretel lay down in them, and thought they were in heaven.

The old woman had only pretended to be so kind; she was in reality a wicked witch, who lay in wait for children, and had only built the little house of bread in order to entice them there. When a child fell into her power, she killed it, cooked and ate it, and that was a feast day with her. Witches have red eyes, and cannot see far, but they have a keen scent like the beasts, and are aware when human beings draw near. When Hansel and Gretel came into her neighbourhood, she laughed with malice, and said mockingly: "I have them, they shall not escape me again!" Early in the morning before the children were awake, she was already up, and when she saw both of them sleeping and looking so pretty, with their plump and rosy cheeks, she muttered to herself: "That will be a dainty mouthful!" Then she seized Hansel with her shrivelled hand, carried him into a little stable, and locked him in behind a grated door. Scream as he might, it would not help him. Then she went to Gretel, shook her till she awoke, and cried: "Get up, lazy thing, fetch some water, and cook something good for your brother, he is in the stable outside, and is to be made fat. When he is fat, I will eat him." Gretel began to weep bitterly, but it was all in vain, for she was forced to do what the wicked witch commanded.

And now the best food was cooked for poor Hansel, but Gretel got nothing but crab-shells. Every morning the woman crept to the little stable, and cried: "Hansel, stretch out your finger that I may feel if you will soon be fat." Hansel, however, stretched out a little bone to her, and the old woman, who had dim eyes, could not see it, and thought it was Hansel's finger, and was astonished that there was no way of fattening him. When four weeks had gone by, and Hansel still remained thin, she was seized with impatience and would not wait any longer. "Now, then, Gretel," she cried to the girl, "stir yourself, and bring some water. Let Hansel be fat or lean, tomorrow I will kill him, and cook him." Ah, how the poor little sister did lament when she had to fetch the water, and how her tears did flow down her cheeks! "Dear God, do help us," she cried. "If the wild beasts in the forest had but devoured us, we should at any rate have died together." "Just keep your noise to yourself," said the old woman, "it won't help you at all."

Early in the morning, Gretel had to go out and hang up the cauldron with the water, and light the fire. "We will bake first," said the old woman, "I have already heated the oven, and kneaded the dough." She pushed poor Gretel out to the oven, from which flames of fire were already darting. "Creep in," said the witch, "and see if it is properly heated, so that we can put the bread in." And once Gretel was inside, she intended to shut the oven and let her bake in it, and then she would eat her, too. But Gretel saw what she had in mind, and said: "I do not know how I am to do it; how do I get in?" "Silly goose," said the old woman. "The door is big enough; just look, I can get in myself!" and she crept up and thrust her head into the oven. Then Gretel gave her a push that drove her far into it, and shut the iron door, and fastened the bolt. Oh! then she began to howl quite horribly, but Gretel ran away and the godless witch was miserably burnt to death.

Gretel, however, ran like lightning to Hansel, opened his little stable, and cried: "Hansel, we are saved! The old witch is dead!" Then Hansel sprang like a bird from its cage when the door is opened. How they did rejoice and embrace each other, and dance about and kiss each other! And as they had no longer any need to fear her, they went into the witch's house, and in every corner there stood chests full of pearls and jewels. "These are far better than pebbles!" said Hansel, and thrust into his pockets whatever could be got in, and Gretel said: "I, too, will take something home with me," and filled her pinafore full. "But now we must be off," said Hansel, "that we may get out of the witch's forest."

When they had walked for two hours, they came to a great stretch of water. "We cannot cross," said Hansel, "I see no foot-plank, and no bridge." "And there is also no ferry," answered Gretel, "but a white duck is swimming there: if I ask her, she will help us over." Then she cried:

> *"Little duck, little duck, dost thou see,*
> *Hansel and Gretel are waiting for thee?*
> *There's never a plank, or bridge in sight,*
> *Take us across on thy back so white."*

The duck came to them, and Hansel seated himself on its back, and told his sister to sit by him. "No," replied Gretel, "that will be too heavy for the little duck; she shall take us across, one after the other." The good little duck did so, and when they were once safely across and had walked for a short time, the forest seemed to be more and more familiar to them, and at length they saw from afar their father's house. Then they began to run, rushed into the parlour, and threw themselves round their father's neck. The man had not known one happy hour since he had left the children in the forest; the woman, however, was dead. Gretel emptied her pinafore until pearls and precious stones ran about the room, and Hansel threw one handful after another out of his pocket to add to them. Then all anxiety was at an end, and they lived together in perfect happiness. My tale is done, there runs a mouse; whosoever catches it, may make himself a big fur cap out of it.

SKILL LEVEL
Easy

Things you'll need:

THE YARN

Super Saver Economy® by Red Heart®,
7oz/198g skeins, each approx 364yds/333m

* 1 skein in #336 Warm Brown (A)

* 1 skein in #316 Soft White (B)

* 1 skein in #505 Aruba Sea (C)

* 1 skein in #706 Perfect Pink (D)

* 1 skein in #672 Spring Green (E)

* 1 skein in #235 Lemon (F)

* 1 skein in #313 Aran (G)

* 1 skein in #319 Cherry Red (H)

* 1 skein in #886 Blue (I)

* 1 skein in #661 Frosty Green (J)

* 1 skein in #3950 Charcoal (K)

* 1 skein in #312 Black (L)

THE HOOK

Size G/6 (4mm) crochet hook

THINGS FOR ALL

Yarn needle
Polyfil stuffing
2 black safety eyes 8mm for Witch
4 black safety eyes 6mm for Hansel and
 Gretel

MEASUREMENTS

Hansel 3½"/9cm tall
Gretel 3½"/9cm tall excluding hair
Witch 5½"/14cm tall excluding hair
Gingerbread House 10 x 6½"/25.5 x 16.5cm

GAUGE

Gauge is not critical.

HANSEL

Head

With G, ch 3, join with sl st to form ring.

Rnd 1: Ch 1, sc 6 into ring, sl st in beg ch.

Inc rnd 2: Ch 1, 2 sc in each st around, sl st in first sc of rnd—12 sc.

Inc rnd 3: Ch 1, *2 sc in first st, sc in next st; rep from * around, sl st in first st of rnd—18 sc.

Rnds 4–7: Ch 1, sc in each st around, sl st in first st of rnd.

Place safety eyes between rnds 4 and 5, 2 sc apart.

Dec rnd 8: Ch 1, *sc2tog, sc in next st; rep from * around, sl st in first st of rnd—12 sc. Stuff head with polyfil.

Dec rnd 9: Ch 1, [sc2tog] 6 times, sl st in first st of rnd—6 sc.

Body

Switch to I.

Inc rnd 10: Ch 1, *2 sc in first st, sc in next st; rep from * around, sl st in first st of rnd—9 sc.

Inc rnd 11: Ch 1, *2 sc in first st, sc in next 2 sts; rep from * around, sl st in first st of rnd—12 sc.

Inc rnd 12: Ch 1, *2 sc in first st, sc in next 3 sts; rep from * around, sl st in first st of rnd—15 sc.

Rnds 13 and 14: Ch 1, sc in each st around, sl st in first st of rnd.

Pants

Switch to H.

Rnd 15: Ch 1, sc in each st around, sl st in first st of rnd.

Dec rnd 16: Ch 1, *sc2tog, sc in next st; rep from * around, sl st in first st of rnd—10 sc.

Dec rnd 17: Ch 1, [sc2tog] 5 times, sl st in first st of rnd—5 sc.

Fasten off, leaving long tail. Thread tail through yarn needle, and weave around rem small opening. Pull tight to cinch closed.

Arms (make 2)

With G, ch 2, 4 sc in first ch, join with sl st to form ring.

Rnd 1: Ch 1, sc in each st around, sl st in first st of rnd.

Switch to I.

Rnds 2–4: Ch 1, sc in each st around, sl st in first st of rnd.

Fasten off.

Legs (make 2)

With I, ch 3, join with sl st to form ring.

Rnd 1: Ch 1, 6 sc in ring, sl st in beg ch.

Rnd 2: Ch 1, sc in each st around, sl st in first st of rnd.

Switch to H.

Rnd 3: Ch 1, sc in each st around, sl st in first st of rnd.

Fasten off.

Finishing Hansel

With B and yarn needle, stitch 2 X's onto front of shirt as shown in photo on page 11.

Stuff Arms and Legs with small amounts of polyfil. Stuff yarn ends into limbs instead of cutting or weaving in, to help fill in limbs and use less stuffing. Leave about top third of arms unstuffed so they lie closer to body. Sew Arms to either side of Body with tall side of Arm Cap at top next to neck. Sew Legs to Body; do not pinch opening closed—sew around edge keeping circular shape intact.

Hair

Cut long strand of A. Using photo as a guide, sew hair onto top of head with long stitches. Start at bottom back of head and work your way up, eventually making long stitches across top of head to form side part.

GRETEL

Head

With G, ch 3, join with sl st to form ring.

Rnd 1: Ch 1, 6 sc in ring, sl st in beg ch.

Inc rnd 2: Ch 1, 2 sc in each st around, sl st in first st of rnd—12 sc.

Inc rnd 3: Ch 1, *2 sc in first st, sc in next st; rep from * around, sl st in first st of rnd—18 sc.

Rnds 4–7: Ch 1, sc in each st around, sl st in first st of rnd.

Place safety eyes between rnds 4 and 5, 2 sc apart.

Dec rnd 8: Ch 1, *sc2tog, sc in next st; rep from * around, sl st in first st of rnd—12 sts. Stuff head with polyfil.

Dec rnd 9: Ch 1, [sc2tog] 6 times, sl st in first st of rnd—6 sc.

Body

Switch to H.

Inc rnd 10: Ch 1, *2 sc in first st, sc in next st; rep from * around, sl st in first st of rnd—9 sc.

Inc rnd 11: Ch 1, *2 sc in first st, sc in next 2 sts; rep from * around, sl st in first st of rnd—12 sc.

Inc rnd 12: Ch 1, *2 sc in first st, sc in next 3 sts; rep from * around, sl st in first st of rnd—15 sc.

Rnds 13–16: Ch 1, sc in each st around, sl st in first st of rnd.

Inc rnd 17: Ch 1, *2 sc in first st, sc in next 4 sts; rep from * around, sl st in first st of rnd—18 sc.

Inc rnd 18: Ch 1, *2 sc in first st, sc in next 5 sts; rep from * around, sl st in first st of rnd—21 sc.

Inc rnd 19: Ch 1, *2 sc in first st, sc in next 6 sts; rep from * around, sl st in first st of rnd—24 sc.

Fasten off.

Base

With H, ch 3, join with sl st to form ring.

Rnd 1: Ch 1, 6 sc in ring, sl st in beg ch.

Inc rnd 2: Ch 1, 2 sc in each st around, sl st in first st of rnd—12 sts.

Inc rnd 3: Ch 1, *2 sc in first st, sc in next st; rep from * around, sl st in first st of rnd—18 sts.

Inc rnd 4: Ch 1, *2 sc in first st, sc in next 2 sts; rep from * around, sl st in first st of rnd—24 sts.

Fasten off.

Arms (make 2)

With G, ch 2, 4 sc in first ch, join with sl st to form ring.

Rnd 1: Ch 1, sc in each st around, sl st in first st of rnd.

Switch to H.

Rnds 2–4: Ch 1, sc in each st around, sl st in first st of rnd.

Fasten off.

Hair

With F, cut 30 strands, each 10" (25.5cm) long. Using photo on page 12 as a guide and yarn needle, attach strands to head along center. Make 2 braids. With I, tie ends of braids.

Apron

With B, ch 7, tr in third ch from hook and in each ch across.

Fasten off, leaving long tail.

Finishing Gretel

Stuff Arms with small amounts of polyfil. Stuff yarn ends into Arms instead of cutting or weaving in, to help fill in Arms and use less stuffing. Leave about top third of Arms unstuffed so they lie closer to Body. Sew Arms to either side of Body with tall side of Arm Cap at top next to neck.

Take Gretel and Base, with wrong sides facing each other; place Gretel in front and Base in back, insert hook into one st and corresponding st on other piece, sc pieces tog. Start at beg/end of rnds, work around leaving small opening. Stuff Body with polyfil, continue sc around. Fasten off.

Note Don't overstuff bottom so that base doesn't curve outward. Bottom should lie flat.

With I and yarn needle, stitch 2 X's onto front of shirt as shown in photo on page 12.

Using photo as a guide, sew apron to body with long tail at top left of apron by right arm. Use tail to form waist tie by wrapping around, sew at back and knot tail to form ties. Wrap to other front and sew apron down by left arm. Wrap end around neck to form neck tie.

WITCH

Head

With J, ch 3, join with sl st to form ring.

Rnd 1: Ch 1, 6 sc in ring, sl st in beg ch.

Inc rnd 2: Ch 1, 2 sc in each st around, sl st in first st of rnd—12 sc.

Inc rnd 3: Ch 1, *2 sc in first st, sc in next st; rep from * around, sl st in first st of rnd—18 sc.

Inc rnd 4: Ch 1, *2 sc in first st, sc in next 2 sts; rep from * around, sl st in first st of rnd—24 sc.

Inc rnd 5: Ch 1, *2 sc in first st, sc in next 3 sts; rep from * around, sl st in first st of rnd—30 sc.

Rnds 6–11: Ch 1, sc in each st around, sl st in first st of rnd.

Place safety eyes between rnds 7 and 8, 4 sts apart.

Dec rnd 12: Ch 1, *sc2tog, sc in next 3 sts; rep from * around, sl st in first st of rnd—24 sc.

Dec rnd 13: Ch 1, *sc2tog, sc in next 2 sts; rep from * around, sl st in first st of rnd—18 sc.

Dec rnd 14: Ch 1, *sc2tog, sc in next st; rep from * around, sl st in first st of rnd—12 sc. Stuff head.

Inc rnd 15: Ch 1, *2 sc in first st, sc in next 2 sts; rep from * around, sl st in first st of rnd—16 sc.

Body

Switch to K.

Inc rnd 16: Ch 1, *2 sc in first st, sc in next 3 sts; rep from * around, sl st in first st of rnd—20 sc.

Inc rnd 17: Ch 1, *2 sc in first st, sc in next 4 sts; rep from * around, sl st in first st of rnd—24 sc.

Rnds 18–25: Ch 1, sc in each st around, sl st in first st of rnd.

Inc rnd 26: Ch 1, *2 sc in first st, sc in next 3 sts; rep from * around, sl st in first st of rnd—30 sc.

Rnd 27: Ch 1, sc in each st around, sl st in first st of rnd.

Inc rnd 28: Ch 1, *2 sc in first st, sc in next 4 sts; rep from * around, sl st in first st of rnd—36 sc.

Rnd 29: Ch 1, sc in each st around, sl st in first st of rnd.

Inc rnd 30: Ch 1, *2 sc in first st, sc in next 3 sts; rep from * around, sl st in first st of rnd—45 sc.

Fasten off.

Base

With K, ch 3, join with sl st to form ring.

Rnd 1: Ch 1, 6 sc in ring, sl st in beg ch.

Inc rnd 2: Ch 1, 2 sc in each st around, sl st in first st of rnd—12 sc.

Inc rnd 3: Ch 1, *2 sc in first st, sc in next st; rep from * around, sl st in first st of rnd—18 sc.

Inc rnd 4: Ch 1, *2 sc in first st, sc in next 2 sts; rep from * around, sl st in first st of rnd—24 sc.

Inc rnd 5: Ch 1, *2 sc in first st, sc in next 3 sts; rep from * around, sl st in first st of rnd—30 sc.

Inc rnd 6: Ch 1, *2 sc in first st, sc in next 4 sts; rep from * around, sl st in first st of rnd—36 sc.

Inc rnd 7: Ch 1, *2 sc in first st, sc in next 3 sts; rep from * around, sl st in first st of rnd—45 sc.

Fasten off.

Arms (make 2)

With J, ch 3, join with sl st to form ring.

Rnd 1: Ch 1, 6 sc in ring, sl st in beg ch.

Inc rnd 2: Ch 1, 2 sc in each st around, sl st in first st of rnd—12 sc.

Rnd 3: Ch 1, sc in each st around, sl st in first st of rnd.

Switch to K.

Rnd 4: Ch 1, sc in each st around, sl st in first st of rnd.

Dec rnd 5: Ch 1, sc2tog, sc around, sl st in first st of rnd—11 sc.

Dec rnd 6: Ch 1, sc2tog, sc around, sl st in first st of rnd—10 sc.

Dec rnd 7: Ch 1, sc2tog, sc around, sl st in first st of rnd—9 sc.

Dec rnd 8: Ch 1, sc2tog, sc around, sl st in first st of rnd—8 sc.

Rnd 9 (arm cap): Ch 1, [sl st in next st] twice, sc in next st, [dc in next st] twice, sc in next st, [sl st in next st] twice, sl st in first st of rnd.

Fasten off.

Finishing Witch

Stuff Arms with small amounts of polyfil. Stuff yarn ends into Arms instead of cutting or weaving in, to help fill in Arms and use less stuffing. Leave about top third of Arms unstuffed so they lie closer to Body. Sew Arms to either side of Body with tall side of Arm Cap at top next to neck.

Take Witch and Base, with wrong sides facing each other; place Witch in front and Base in back

and insert hook into one st and corresponding st on other piece, sc pieces tog. Start at beg/end of rnds and work around, leaving small opening. Stuff Body with polyfil; continue sc around. Fasten off.

Note Don't overstuff bottom—so that base doesn't curve outward. Bottom should lie flat.

Witch Hair

Cut 20 strands each of J, K and L 6"/15cm long. Using photo as a guide and yarn needle, attach strands to head along center, alternating colors. Cut more strands or use fewer strands as needed.

GINGERBREAD HOUSE

Side (make 2)

With A, ch 35.

Row 1 (RS): Sc into second ch from hook and in each rem ch across—34 sc.

Row 2 (WS): Ch 1, turn, sc into each st across.

Row 3: Ch 1, turn, sc into each st across.

Repeat rows 2 and 3 for 17 times more.

Fasten off.

Front/Back (make 2)

Ch 26.

Row 1 (RS): Sc into second ch from hook and in each rem ch across—25 sc.

Row 2 (WS): Ch 1, turn, sc into each st scross.

Row 3 (RS): Ch 1, turn, sc into each st across.

Rep rows 2 and 3 for 17 times.

Next dec row: Ch 1, turn, sc2tog, sc across to last 2 sts, sc2tog—2 sts dec'd.

Rep last row for 10 times more—3 sc. Fasten off.

Bottom

Ch 26.

Row 1 (RS): Sc into second ch from hook and in each rem ch across—25 sc.

Row 2 (WS): Ch 1, turn, sc into each st across.

Row 3 (RS): Ch 1, turn, sc into each st across.

Rep rows 2 and 3 for 19 times more. Rep row 2 once more. Fasten off.

Roof Top Strip
Ch 5.

Row 1 (RS): Sc into second ch from hook and in each rem ch across—4 sc.

Row 2 (WS): Ch 1, turn, sc into each st across.

Row 3 (RS): Ch 1, turn, sc into each st across.

Rep rows 2 and 3 for 19 times more. Rep row 2 once more. Fasten off.

Roof Sides (make 2)
Ch 37.

Row 1 (RS): Sc into second ch from hook and in each rem ch across—36 sc.

Row 2 (WS): Ch 1, turn, sc into each st across.

Row 3 (RS): Ch 1, turn, sc into each st across.

Rep rows 2 and 3 for 16 times more. Rep row 2 once more. Fasten off.

Roof Edging

Sides (Make 2)

Ch 37.

Next row: Sc in second ch from hook and in each st across—36 sts.

Next row: Ch 1, *sk next st, 4 dc in next st (shell made), sk next st, sc in next st; rep from * to end.

Fasten off.

Front/Back (make 2)

With B, ch 46.

Next row: Sc in second ch from hook and in next 18 sts, sc2tog, sc in next 3 sts, sc2tog, sc 19—43 sts.

Next row: Ch 1, [sc, sk 1, shell, sk 1] 5 times, sc, sk 1, sc, [sk 1, shell, sk 1, sc] 5 times.

Fasten off.

Gumball Spires

Note Make 3 in D, 2 in C, 2 in E and 2 in F.

Ch 3, join with sl st to form ring.

Rnd 1: Ch 1, 6 sc in ring, sl st in beg ch.

Inc rnd 2: Ch 1, 2 sc in each st around, sl st in first st of rnd—12 sc.

Rnds 3 and 4: Ch 1, sc in each st around, sl st in first st of rnd. Stuff slightly.

Piece Roof Together

Take Top Strip and Roof Side, with wrong sides facing each other, and Top Strip in front and Roof Side in back—insert hook into one st and corresponding st on other piece, sc pieces tog.

Fasten off. Rep with Top Strip and other Roof side.

Sc Roof Edging pieces onto roof onto appropriate sides with wrong sides facing each other; insert hook into one st and corresponding st on other piece, sc pieces tog. After Roof Edging pieces are attached, sew edges of pieces tog.

Sew gumball spires on Roof. Starting at front in foll order: D, F, E, C, D, F, E, C, D.

Door

With C, ch 9.

Row 1 (RS): Sc into second ch from hook and into each ch across—8 sc.

Row 2 (WS): Ch 1, turn, sc into each st across.

Rep row 2 for 12 times more.

Row 15: Ch 1, turn, sc in next st, hdc in next st, dc in next st, [tr in next st] twice, dc in next st, hdc in next st, sc in next st.

Fasten off.

Windows (make 2)

With B, ch 3, join with sl st to form ring.

Rnd 1: Ch 1, 6 sc in ring, sl st in beg ch.

Inc rnd 2: Ch 1, 2 sc in each st around, sl st in first st of rnd—12 sc.

Inc rnd 3: Ch 1, *2 sc in first st, sc in next st; rep from * around, sl st in first st of rnd—18 sc.

Fasten off.

Candy Pieces

Note Make 3 of each shape with colors C, D, E, F.

Circles

Ch 3, join with sl st to form ring.

Rnd 1: Ch 1, 6 sc in ring, sl st in beg ch.

Rnd 2: Ch 1, 2 sc in each st around, sl st in first st of rnd—12 sc.

Fasten off.

Triangle

Ch 3, join with sl st to form ring.

Rnd 1: Ch 1, 6 sc in ring, sl st in beg ch.

Inc rnd 2: Ch 1, *2 sc into next st, 2 dc into next st; rep from * around, sl st in first st of rnd—9 sc.

Fasten off.

Square

Ch 5.

Row 1: Sc in second ch from hook and in each ch across—4 sc.

Row 2: Ch 1, turn, sc in each st across.

Rep row 2 twice more. Fasten off.

Finishing Gingerbread House

Using photo on page 16 as guide, sew windows and door onto front. With B and yarn needle, embroider window onto door. With C, embroider vertical and horizontal lines onto window.

Randomly choosing from candy pieces, sew 8 pieces to Front, 6 to each Roof Side and 8 to each House Side. With B, randomly make french knots onto House to fill in empty spaces between candy pieces.

Note: All House Pieces are worked bottom up; this is how you know which side is which.

Take two House Pieces, with wrong sides facing each other—insert hook into one st and corresponding st on other piece, sc pieces tog. Fasten off and rep with rem House Pieces, saving Bottom Pieces to be attached last.

Sew roof onto house, stuffing with polyfil when one edge remains to be sewn.

Optional Leave one side of roof open in order to store characters inside.

The Hare and the Hedgehog

This story, my dear young folks, seems to be false, but it really is true, for my grandfather, from whom I have it, used always, when relating it, to say complacently, "It must be true, my son, or else no one could tell it to you." The story is as follows. One Sunday morning about harvest time, just as the buckwheat was in bloom, the sun was shining brightly in heaven, the east wind was blowing warmly over the stubble-fields, the larks were singing in the air, the bees buzzing among the buckwheat, the people were all going in their Sunday clothes to church, and all creatures were happy, and the hedgehog was happy too.

The hedgehog, however, was standing by his door with his arms akimbo, enjoying the morning breezes, and slowly trilling a little song to himself, which was neither better nor worse than the songs which hedgehogs are in the habit of singing on a blessed Sunday morning. Whilst he was thus singing half aloud to himself, it suddenly occurred to him that, while his wife was washing and drying the children, he might very well take a walk into the field, and see how his turnips were going on. The turnips were, in fact, close beside his house, and he and his family were accustomed to eat them, for which reason he looked upon them as his own. No sooner said than done. The hedgehog shut the house-door behind him, and took the path to the field. He had not gone very far from home, and was just turning round the sloe-bush which stands there outside the field, to go up into the turnip-field, when he observed the hare who had gone out on business of the same kind, namely, to visit his cabbages. When the hedgehog caught sight of the hare, he bade him a friendly good morning. But the hare, who was in his own way a distinguished gentleman, and frightfully haughty, did not return the hedgehog's greeting, but said to him, assuming at the same time a very contemptuous manner, "How do you happen to be running about here in the field so early in the morning?" — "I am taking a walk," said the hedgehog. "A walk!" said the hare, with a smile. "It seems to me that you might use your legs for a better purpose." This answer made the hedgehog furiously angry, for he can bear anything but an attack on his legs, just because they are crooked by nature. So now the hedgehog said to the hare, "You seem to imagine that you can do more with your legs than I with mine." — "That is just what I do think," said the hare. "That can be put to the test," said the hedgehog. "I wager that if we run a race, I will outstrip you." — "That is ridiculous! You with your short legs!" said the hare, "but for my part I am willing, if you have such a monstrous fancy for it. What shall we wager?" — "A golden louis-d'or and a bottle of brandy," said the hedgehog. "Done," said the hare. "Shake hands on it, and then we may as well come off at once." — "Nay," said the hedgehog, "there is no such great hurry! I am still fasting, I will go home first, and have a little breakfast. In half-an-hour I will be back again at this place."

Hereupon the hedgehog departed, for the hare was quite satisfied with this. On his way the hedgehog thought to himself, "The hare relies on his long legs, but I will contrive to get the better of him. He may be a great man, but he is a very silly fellow, and he shall pay for what he has said." So when the hedgehog reached home, he said to his wife, "Wife, dress thyself quickly, thou must go out to the field with me." — "What is going on, then?" said his wife. "I have made a wager with the hare, for a gold louis-d'or and a bottle of brandy. I am to run a race with him, and thou must be present." — "Good heavens, husband," the wife now cried, "art thou not right in thy mind, hast thou completely lost thy wits? What can make thee want to run a race with the hare?" — "Hold thy tongue, woman," said the hedgehog, "that is my affair. Don't begin

22

to discuss things which are matters for men. Be off, dress thyself, and come with me." What could the hedgehog's wife do? She was forced to obey him, whether she liked it or not.

So when they had set out on their way together, the hedgehog said to his wife, "Now pay attention to what I am going to say. Look you, I will make the long field our race-course. The hare shall run in one furrow, and I in another, and we will begin to run from the top. Now all that thou hast to do is to place thyself here below in the furrow, and when the hare arrives at the end of the furrow, on the other side of thee, thou must cry out to him, 'I am here already!'"

Then they reached the field, and the hedgehog showed his wife her place, and then walked up the field. When he reached the top, the hare was already there. "Shall we start?" said the hare. "Certainly," said the hedgehog. "Then both at once." So saying, each placed himself in his own furrow. The hare counted, "Once, twice, thrice, and away!" and went off like a whirlwind down the field. The hedgehog, however, only ran about three paces, and then he stooped down in the furrow, and stayed quietly where he was. When the hare therefore arrived in full career at the lower end of the field, the hedgehog's wife met him with the cry, "I am here already!" The hare was shocked and wondered not a little, he thought no other than that it was the hedgehog himself who was calling to him, for the hedgehog's wife looked just like her husband. The hare, however, thought to himself, "That has not been done fairly," and cried, "It must be run again, let us have it again." And once more he went off like the wind in a storm, so that he seemed to fly. But the hedgehog's wife stayed quietly in her place. So when the hare reached the top of the field, the hedgehog himself cried out to him, "I am here already." The hare, however, quite beside himself with anger, cried, "It must be run again, we must have it again." — "All right," answered the hedgehog, "for my part we'll run as often as you choose." So the hare ran seventy-three times more, and the hedgehog always held out against him, and every time the hare reached either the top or the bottom, either the hedgehog or his wife said, "I am here already."

At the seventy-fourth time, however, the hare could no longer reach the end. In the middle of the field he fell to the ground, blood streamed out of his mouth, and he lay dead on the spot. But the hedgehog took the louis-d'or which he had won and the bottle of brandy, called his wife out of the furrow, and both went home together in great delight, and if they are not dead, they are living there still.

This is how it happened that the hedgehog made the hare run races with him on the Buxtehuder heath till he died, and since that time no hare has ever had any fancy for running races with a Buxtehuder hedgehog.

The moral of this story, however, is, firstly, that no one, however great he may be, should permit himself to jest at any one beneath him, even if he be only a hedgehog. And, secondly, it teaches, that when a man marries, he should take a wife in his own position, who looks just as he himself looks. So whosoever is a hedgehog let him see to it that his wife is a hedgehog also, and so forth.

SKILL LEVEL

Easy

Things you'll need:

THE YARN

For Hare and Hedgehogs

Fisherman's Wool® by Lion Brand® Yarn, 8oz/227g skeins, each approx 465yds/425m

* 1 skein in #098 Natural (A)

For Hedgehogs

Martha Stewart Crafts™/MC Glitter Eyelash by Lion Brand® Yarn, .88oz/25g skeins, each approx 39yds/35m

* 1 skein in #526 Brownstone (B)

For Carrot

Vanna's Choice® by Lion Brand® Yarn, 3½oz/100g skeins, each approx 170yds/156m

* 1 skein in #134 Terracotta (C)

* 1 skein in #171 Fern (D)

THE HOOKS

Size G/6 (4mm) crochet hook
Size H/8 (5mm) crochet hook

THINGS FOR ALL

Polyfil Stuffing

Yarn Needle

3 black safety eyes 8mm for Hare

6 black safety eyes 6mm for Hedgehogs

MEASUREMENTS

Hare 6¼"/16cm tall when sitting and ears straight up
Carrot 3½"/9cm including top
Roly Poly Hedgehog 3½"/9cm long
Standing Hedgehog 3½"/9cm long

GAUGE

Gauge is not critical.

ROLY POLY HEDGEHOG

Head

With A and smaller hook, ch 3, join with sl st to form ring.

Rnd 1: Ch 1, 6 sc in ring, sl st in beg ch.

Rnd 2: Ch 1, sc in each st around, sl st in first st of rnd.

Inc rnd 3: Ch 1, *[2 sc in next st] twice, sc in next st; rep from * around, sl st in first st of rnd—10 sc.

Inc rnd 4: Ch 1, *2 sc in next st, sc in next st, 2 sc in next st, sc in next 2 sts; rep from * around, sl st in first st of rnd—14 sc.

Inc rnd 5: Ch 1, *2 sc in next st, sc in next 2 sts, 2 sc in next st, sc in next 3 sts; rep from * around, sl st in first st of rnd—18 sc.

Inc rnd 6: Ch 1, *2 sc in next st, sc in next 2 sts; rep from * around, sl st in first st of rnd—24 sc.

Rnds 7 and 8: Ch 1, sc in each st around, sl st in first st of rnd.

Switch to B and larger hook.

Rnd 9: Ch 1, sc in each st around, sl st in first st of rnd.

Dec rnd 10: Ch 1, *sc2tog, sc in next 2 sts; rep from * around, sl st in first st of rnd—18 sc.

Place 2 safety eyes between rnds 5 and 6, 3 sts apart; 1 for nose tip in first 6 sc rnd.

Dec rnd 11: Ch 1, *sc2tog, sc in next st; rep from * around, sl st in first st of rnd—12 sc.

Stuff the head with polyfil.

Rnd 12: Ch 1, sc2tog around, sl st in first st of rnd—6 sts.

Fasten off, leaving long tail. Thread tail through needle, weave around rem small opening. Pull tight to cinch closed.

Body

With A and smaller hook, ch 3, join with sl st to form ring.

Rnd 1: Ch 1, 6 sc in ring, sl st in beg ch.

Inc rnd 2: Ch 1, [2 sc in next st] twice, [2 dc in next st] twice, [2 sc in next st] twice, sl st in first st of rnd—8 sc, 4 dc.

Inc rnd 3: Ch 1, [2 sc in next st, sc in next st] twice, [2 dc in next st, dc in next st] twice, [2 sc in next st, sc in next st] twice, sl st in first st of rnd—12 sc, 6dc.

Switch to B.

Inc rnd 4: Ch 1, 2 dc in next st, dc in next 2 sts, [2 sc in next st, sc in next 2 sts] 4 times, 2 dc in next st, dc in next 2 sts, sl st in first st of rnd—16 sc, 8 dc.

Rnds 5–7: Ch 1, sc in each st around, sl st in first st of rnd.

Dec rnd 8: Ch 1, *sc2tog, sc in next 2 sts; rep from * around, sl st in first st of rnd—18 sc.

Stuff body, pressing thumb into center of belly; stuff around your thumb to make donut shape with less stuffing in center of body. This will help belly to become more concave and make the hedge look more roly poly. Add more stuffing after next dec rnds if needed.

Rnd 9: Ch 1, *sc2tog, sc in next st; rep from * around, sl st in first st of rnd—12 sc.

Rnd 10: Ch 1, sc2tog around, sl st in first st of rnd—6 sts.

Fasten off, leaving long tail. Thread tail through yarn needle, weave around rem small opening. Pull tight to cinch closed. Sew head to body.

STANDING HEDGEHOG

Head

With A and smaller hook, ch 3, join with sl st to form ring.

Rnd 1: Ch 1, 6 sc in ring, sl st in beg ch.

Rnd 2: Ch 1, sc in each st around, sl st in first st of rnd.

Inc rnd 3: Ch 1, *[2 sc in next st] twice, sc in next st, rep from * around, sl st in first st of rnd—10 sc.

Inc rnd 4: Ch 1, *2 sc in next st, sc in next st, 2 sc in next st, sc in next 2 sts; rep from * around, sl st in first st of rnd—14 sc.

Inc rnd 5: Ch 1, *2 sc in next st, sc in next 2 sts, 2 sc in next st, sc in next 3 sts; rep from * around, sl st in first st of rnd—18 sc.

Inc rnd 6: Ch 1, *2 sc in next st, sc in next 2 sts; rep from * around, sl st in first st—24 sc.

Fasten off. Place 2 safety eyes between rnds 5 and 6, 3 sts apart; 1 for nose tip in first 6 sc rnd.

Belly

With A, smaller hook and RS facing of Head, rejoin yarn 4 sts from beg of last rnd.

Next row: Ch 1, sc in next 4 sts, sc in next 5 st skipping over sl st, ch 1 from last rnd of head—9 sts.

Next row: Ch 1, turn, sc in each st across.

Rep last row 10 times more, or until hedge belly measures about 2"/5cm long from joining row.

Back

With larger hook and RS facing, join B in edge of belly right next to head. Work sc in each open st around head, sl st in opposite belly edge—15 sc.

Next row: Ch 1, turn, sc in each st across, sl st in belly edge next to previous join.

Work last row 10 times more, or until back measures same as belly.

Next row: Sc across 9 sts of belly and join with sl st in first st of last back row, skipping previous sl st—24 sts.

Next dec rnd: Ch 1, *sc2tog, sc in next 2 sts; rep from * around, sl st in first st of rnd—18 sc.

Next dec rnd: Ch 1, *sc2tog, sc in next st; rep from * around, sl st in first st of rnd—12 sc.

Stuff body with polyfil.

Next dec rnd: Ch 1, sc2tog around, sl st in first st of rnd—6 sc. Fasten off.

FOR BOTH HEDGEHOGS

Ears (make 4)

With A, ch 3, dc in second ch from hook and in last ch. Fasten off.

Legs (make 8)

Using A and smaller hook, ch 3, join with sl st to form ring.

Rnd 1: Ch 1, 6 sc in ring, sl st in beg ch.

Rnd 2: Ch 1, sc in each st around, sl st in first st of rnd.

Fasten off.

Finishing Hedgehogs

Stuff Legs with small amounts of polyfil. Stuff yarn ends into legs instead of cutting or weaving in, to help fill in the limbs and use less stuffing. Sew Legs to belly; do not pinch opening closed—sew around edge, keeping circular shape intact.

Sew Ears to top of Head above eyes.

HARE

Head

With A and smaller hook, ch 3, join with sl st to form ring.

Rnd 1: Ch 1, 6 sc in ring, sl st in beg ch.

Rnd 2: Ch 1, sc in each st around, sl st in first st of rnd.

Inc rnd 3: Ch 1, *[2 sc in next st] twice, sc in next st; rep from * around, sl st in first st of rnd—10 sc.

Inc rnd 4: Ch 1, *2 sc in next st, sc in next st, 2 sc in next st, sc in next 2 sts; rep from * around, sl st in first st of rnd—14 sc.

Inc rnd 5: Ch 1, *2 sc in next st, sc in next 2 sts, 2 sc in next st, sc in next 3 sts; rep from * around, sl st in first st of rnd—18 sc.

Inc rnd 6: Ch 1, *2 sc in next st, sc in next 2 sts; rep from * around, sl st in first st of rnd—24 sc.

Inc rnd 7: Ch 1, *2 sc in next st, sc in next 3 sts; rep from * around, sl st in first st of rnd—30 sc.

Rnds 8–10: Ch 1, sc in each st around, sl st in first st of rnd.

Dec rnd 11: Ch 1, *sc2tog, sc in next 3 sts; rep from * around, sl st in first st of rnd—24 sc.

Dec rnd 12: Ch 1, *sc2tog, sc in next 2 sts; rep from * around, sl st in first st of rnd—18 sc.

Place 2 safety eyes between rnds 5 and 6, 3 sts apart; 1 for nose tip in first 6 sc rnd.

Dec rnd 13: Ch 1, *sc2tog, sc in next st; rep from * around, sl st in first st of rnd—12 sc.

Stuff body with polyfil.

Dec rnd 14: Ch 1, sc2tog around, sl st in first st of rnd—6 sc.

Fasten off.

Body

With A and smaller hook, ch 16, join with sl st to form ring.

Inc rnd 1: Ch 1, *2 sc in first st, sc in next 3 sts; rep from * around, sl st in first st of rnd—20 sc.

Rnds 2 and 3: Ch 1, sc in each st around, sl st in first st of rnd.

Inc rnd 4: Ch 1, *2 sc in first st, sc in next 4 sts; rep from * around, sl st in first st of rnd—24 sc.

Rnds 5 and 6: Ch 1, sc in each st around, sl st in first st of rnd.

Inc rnd 7: [2 sc in next st, sc in next st] twice, 2 sc in next st, sc in next 14 sts, [2 sc in next st, sc in next st] twice, 2 sc in next st, sl st in first st of rnd—30 sc.

Rnds 8–12: Ch 1, sc in each st around, sl st in first st of rnd.

Dec rnd 13: Ch 1, *sc2tog, sc in next 3 sts; rep from * around, sl st in first st of rnd—24 sc.

Dec rnd 14: Ch 1, *sc2tog, sc in next 2 sts; rep from * around, sl st in first st of rnd—18 sc.

Stuff body with polyfil.

Dec rnd 15: Ch 1, *sc2tog, sc in next st; rep from * around, sl st in first st of rnd—12 sc.

Dec rnd 16: Ch 1, sc2tog around, sl st in first st of rnd—6 sc.

Fasten off.

Arms (make 2)

With A and smaller hook, ch 3, join with sl st to form ring.

Rnd 1: Ch 1, 6 sc in ring, sl st in begg ch.

Inc rnd 2: Ch 1, 2 sc in each st around, sl st in first st of rnd—12 sc.

Rnds 3 and 4: Ch 1, sc in each st around, sl st in first st of rnd.

Dec rnd 5: Ch 1, sc2tog around—6 sc.

Rnds 6–11: Ch 1, sc in each st around, sl st in first st of rnd.

Fasten off. Stuff with polyfil.

Legs (make 2)

With A and smaller hook, ch 3, join with sl st to form ring.

Rnd 1: Ch 1, 6 sc in ring, sl st in beg ch.

Inc rnd 2: Ch 1, 2 sc in each st around, sl st in first st of rnd—12 sc.

Inc rnd 3: Ch 1, *2 sc in first st, sc in next st; rep from * around, sl st in first st of rnd—18 sc.

Rnds 4 and 5: Ch 1, sc in each st around, sl st in first st of rnd.

Dec rnd 6: Ch 1, sc2tog around—9 sc.

Rnds 7–10: Ch 1, sc in each st around, sl st in first st of rnd.

Rnd 11: Ch 1, *sc2tog, sc in next st; rep from * around, sl st in first st of rnd—6 sc.

Fasten off.

Stuff with polyfil, leaving top third unstuffed.

Ears

With A and smaller hook, ch 3, join with sl st to form ring.

Rnd 1: Ch 1, 6 sc in ring, sl st in beg ch.

Rnds 2 and 3: Ch 1, sc in each st around, sl st in first st of rnd.

Inc rnd 4: Ch 1, *2 sc in next st, sc in next st; rep from * around—9 sc.

Rnds 5–10: Ch 1, sc in each st around, sl st in first st of rnd.

Dec rnd 11: Ch 1, *sc2tog, sc in next st; rep from * around—6 sc.

Fasten off.

Tail

With A and smaller hook, ch 3, join with sl st to form ring.

Rnd 1: Ch 1, 6 sc in ring, sl st in beg ch.

Rnd 2: Ch 1, sc in each st around, sl st in first st of rnd.

Inc rnd 3: Ch 1, *2 sc in next st, sc in next st; rep from * around—9 sc.

Rnd 4: Ch 1, sc in each st around, sl st in first st of rnd.

Dec rnd 5: Ch 1, *sc2tog, sc in next st; rep from * around—6 sc.

Fasten off.

Carrot
(make as many as desired)

With C and smaller hook, ch 3, join with sl st to form ring.

Rnd 1: Ch 1, 6 sc in ring, sl st in beg ch.

Inc rnd 2: Ch 1, 2 sc in each st around, sl st in first st of rnd—12 sc.

Rnds 3 and 4: Ch 1, sc in each st around, sl st in first st of rnd.

Rnd 5: Ch 1, *sc2tog, sc in next 4 sts; rep from * around—10 sc.

Rnd 6: Ch 1, sc2tog, sc each st around—9 sc.

Rep rnd 6 until 2 sts rem; AT SAME TIME, stuff with polyfil when 8 sts rem and continue to add more stuffing as you work decreases.

Fasten off, leaving long tail and sew tip of carrot closed.

Stem

With D and smaller hook, *ch 12, sl st in first ch; rep from * 3 times more, always placing sl st in same ch. Sew to top of carrot.

Finishing Hare

Using photo on page 28 as a guide, sew Ears to Head and Tail to Body. Sew Arms to either side of Body, just under neck. Sew Legs to Body by flattening top of Leg and sewing underneath Body, pointed outward in a V-shape. Sew Carrot to Arms.

Jack and the Beanstalk

There was once upon a time a poor widow who had an only son named Jack, and a cow named Milky-White. And all they had to live on was the milk the cow gave every morning, which they carried to the market and sold. But one morning Milky-White gave no milk, and they didn't know what to do. "What shall we do, what shall we do?" said the widow, wringing her hands. "Cheer up, mother, I'll go and get work somewhere," said Jack. "We've tried that before, and nobody would take you," said his mother. "We must sell Milky-White and with the money start a shop, or something." "All right, mother," says Jack. "It's market day today, and I'll soon sell Milky-White, and then we'll see what we can do."

So he took the cow's halter in his hand, and off he started. He hadn't gone far when he met a funny-looking old man, who said to him, "Good morning, Jack." "Good morning to you," said Jack, and wondered how he knew his name. "Well, Jack, and where are you off to?" said the man. "I'm going to market to sell our cow there." "Oh, you look the proper sort of chap to sell cows," said the man. "I wonder if you know how many beans make five." "Two in each hand and one in your mouth," says Jack, as sharp as a needle.

"Right you are," says the man, "and here they are, the very beans themselves," he went on, pulling out of his pocket a number of strange-looking beans. "As you are so sharp," says he, "I don't mind doing a swap with you — your cow for these beans." "Go along," says Jack. "Wouldn't you like it?" "Ah! You don't know what these beans are," said the man. "If you plant them overnight, by morning they grow right up to the sky." "Really?" said Jack. "You don't say so." "Yes, that is so. And if it doesn't turn out to be true you can have your cow back." "Right," says Jack, and hands him over Milky-White's halter and pockets the beans.

Back goes Jack home, and as he hadn't gone very far it wasn't dusk by the time he got to his door. "Back already, Jack?" said his mother. "I see you haven't got Milky-White, so you've sold her. How much did you get for her?" "You'll never guess, mother," says Jack. "No, you don't say so. Good boy! Five pounds? Ten? Fifteen? No, it can't be twenty." "I told you you couldn't guess. What do you say to these beans? They're magical. Plant them overnight and — "

"What!" says Jack's mother. "Have you been such a fool, such a dolt, such an idiot, as to give away my Milky-White, the best milker in the parish, and prime beef to boot, for a set of paltry beans? Take that! Take that! Take that! And as for your precious beans here they go out of the window. And now off with you to bed. Not a sup shall you drink, and not a bit shall you swallow this very night."

So Jack went upstairs to his little room in the attic, and sad and sorry he was, to be sure, as much for his mother's sake as for the loss of his supper. At last he dropped off to sleep.

When he woke up, the room looked so funny. The sun was shining into part of it, and yet all the rest was quite dark and shady. So Jack jumped up and dressed himself and went to the window. And what do you think he saw? Why, the beans his mother had thrown out of the window into the garden had sprung up into a big beanstalk which went up and up and up till it reached the sky. So the man spoke truth after all.

The beanstalk grew up quite close past Jack's window, so all he had to do was to open it and give a jump onto the beanstalk which ran up just like a big ladder. So Jack climbed, and he climbed, and he climbed, and he climbed, and he climbed, and he climbed, and he climbed till at last he reached the sky. And when he got there he found a long broad road going as straight as a dart. So he walked along, and he walked along, and he walked along till he came to a great big tall house, and on the doorstep there was a great big tall woman.

"Good morning, mum," says Jack, quite polite-like. "Could you be so kind as to give me some breakfast?" For he hadn't had anything to eat, you know, the night before, and was as hungry as a hunter. "It's breakfast you want, is it?" says the great big tall woman. "It's breakfast you'll be if you don't move off from here. My man is an ogre and there's nothing he likes better than boys broiled on toast. You'd better be moving on or he'll be coming." "Oh! please, mum, do give me something to eat, mum. I've had nothing to eat since yesterday morning, really and truly, mum," says Jack. "I may as well be broiled as die of hunger."

Well, the ogre's wife was not half so bad after all. So she took Jack into the kitchen, and gave him a hunk of bread and cheese and a jug of milk. But Jack hadn't half finished these when thump! thump! thump! the whole house began to tremble with the noise of someone coming. "Goodness gracious me! It's my old man," said the ogre's wife. "What on earth shall I do? Come along quick and jump in here." And she bundled Jack into the oven just as the ogre came in.

He was a big one, to be sure. At his belt he had three calves strung up by the heels, and he unhooked them and threw them down on the table and said, "Here, wife, broil me a couple of these for breakfast. Ah! what's this I smell?

Fee-fi-fo-fum, I smell the blood of an Englishman, Be he alive, or be he dead, I'll have his bones to grind my bread."

"Nonsense, dear," said his wife. "You're dreaming. Or perhaps you smell the scraps of that little boy you liked so much for yesterday's dinner. Here, you go and have a wash and tidy up, and by the time you come back your breakfast'll be ready for you." So off the ogre went, and Jack was just going to jump out of the oven and run away when the woman told him not to. "Wait till he's asleep," says she; "he always has a doze after breakfast." Well, the ogre had his breakfast, and after that he goes to a big chest and takes out a couple of bags of gold, and down he sits and counts till at last his head began to nod and he began to snore till the whole house shook again.

Then Jack crept out on tiptoe from his oven, and as he was passing the ogre, he took one of the bags of gold under his arm, and off he pelters till he came to the beanstalk, and then he threw down the bag of gold, which, of course, fell into his mother's garden, and then he climbed down and climbed down till at last he got home and told his mother and showed her the gold and said, "Well, mother, wasn't I right about the beans? They are really magical, you see."

So they lived on the bag of gold for some time, but at last they came to the end of it, and Jack made up his mind to try his luck once more at the top of the beanstalk. So one fine morning he rose up early, and got onto the beanstalk, and he climbed, and he climbed, and he climbed, and he climbed, and he climbed, and he climbed till at last he came out onto the road again and up to the great tall house he had been to before. There, sure enough, was the great tall woman a-standing on the doorstep.

"Good morning, mum," says Jack, as bold as brass, "could you be so good as to give me something to eat?" "Go away, my boy," said the big tall woman, "or else my man will eat you up for breakfast. But aren't you the youngster who came here once before? Do you know, that very day my man missed one of his bags of gold." "That's strange, mum," said Jack, "I dare say I could tell you something about that, but I'm so hungry I can't speak till I've had something to eat."

Well, the big tall woman was so curious that she took him in and gave him something to eat. But he had scarcely begun munching it as slowly as he could when thump! thump! they heard the giant's footstep, and his wife hid Jack away in the oven. All happened as it did before. In came the ogre as he did before, said, "Fee-fi-fo-fum," and had his breakfast off three broiled oxen. Then he said, "Wife, bring me the hen that lays the golden eggs." So she brought it, and the ogre said, "Lay," and it laid an egg all of gold. And then the ogre began to nod his head, and to snore till the house shook.

Then Jack crept out of the oven on tiptoe and caught hold of the golden hen, and was off before you could say "Jack Robinson." But this time the hen gave a cackle which woke the ogre, and just as Jack got out of the house he heard him calling, "Wife, wife, what have you done with my golden hen?" And the wife said, "Why, my dear?" But that was all Jack heard, for he rushed off to the beanstalk and climbed down like a house on fire. And when he got home he showed his mother the wonderful hen, and said "Lay" to it; and it laid a golden egg every time he said "Lay."

Well, Jack was not content, and it wasn't long before he determined to have another try at his luck up there at the top of the beanstalk. So one fine morning he rose up early and got to the beanstalk, and he climbed, and he climbed, and he climbed, and he climbed till he got to the top. But this time he knew better than to go straight to the ogre's house. And when he got near it, he waited behind a bush till he saw the ogre's wife come out with a pail to get some water, and then he crept into the house and got into the copper. He hadn't been there long when he heard thump! thump! thump! as before, and in came the ogre and his wife.

"Fee-fi-fo-fum, I smell the blood of an Englishman," cried out the ogre. "I smell him, wife, I smell him." "Do you, my dearie?" says the ogre's wife. "Then, if it's that little rogue that stole your gold and the hen that laid the golden eggs he's sure to have got into the oven." And they both rushed to the oven. But Jack wasn't there, luckily, and the ogre's wife said, "There you are again with your fee-fi-fo-fum. Why, of course, it's the boy you caught last night that I've just broiled for your breakfast. How forgetful I am, and how careless you are not to know the difference between live and dead after all these years."

So the ogre sat down to the breakfast and ate it, but every now and then he would mutter, "Well, I could have sworn —" and he'd get up and search the larder and the cupboards and everything, only, luckily, he didn't think of the copper. After breakfast was over, the ogre called out, "Wife, wife, bring me my golden harp." So she brought it and put it on the table before him. Then he said, "Sing!" and the golden harp sang most beautifully. And it went on singing till the ogre fell asleep, and commenced to snore like thunder. Then Jack lifted up the copper lid very quietly and got down like a mouse and crept on hands and knees till he came to the table, when up he crawled, caught hold of the golden harp and dashed with it towards the door. But the harp called out quite loud, "Master! Master!" and the ogre woke up just in time to see Jack running off with his harp.

Jack ran as fast as he could, and the ogre came rushing after, and would soon have caught him, only Jack had a start and dodged him a bit and knew where he was going. When he got to the beanstalk the ogre was not more than twenty yards away when suddenly he saw Jack disappear, and when he came to the end of the road he saw Jack underneath climbing down for dear life. Well, the ogre didn't like trusting himself to such a ladder, and he stood and waited, so Jack got another start. But just then the harp cried out, "Master! Master!" and the ogre swung himself down onto the beanstalk, which shook with his weight. Down climbs Jack, and after him climbed the ogre.

By this time Jack had climbed down and climbed down and climbed down till he was very nearly home. So he called out, "Mother! Mother! bring me an ax, bring me an ax." And his mother came rushing out with the ax in her hand, but when she came to the beanstalk she stood stock still with fright, for there she saw the ogre with his legs just through the clouds.

But Jack jumped down and got hold of the ax and gave a chop at the beanstalk, which cut it in two. The ogre felt the beanstalk shake and quiver, so he stopped to see what was the matter. Then Jack gave another chop with the ax, and the beanstalk was cut in two and began to topple over. Then the ogre fell down and broke his crown, and the beanstalk came toppling after. Then Jack showed his mother his golden harp, and what with showing that and selling the golden eggs, Jack and his mother became very rich, and he married a great princess, and they lived happy ever after.

SKILL LEVEL
Easy

Things you'll need:

THE YARN

For Jack and Beanstalk

Vanna's Choice® by Lion Brand® Yarn, 3½oz/100g skeins, each approx 170yds/156m

* 1 skein in #123 Beige (A)
* 1 skein in #171 Fern (B)
* 1 skein in #107 Sapphire (C)
* 1 skein in #153 Black (D)
* 1 skein in #130 Honey (E)
* 1 skein in #172 Kelly Green (F)
* 1 skein in #304 Seaspray Mist (G)

For Giant

Wool-Ease® Thick & Quick® by Lion Brand® Yarn, 6oz/170g skeins, each approx 106yds/97m

* 1 skein in #098 Linen (H)
* 1 skein in #138 Cranberry (I)
* 1 skein in #110 Navy (J)
* 1 skein in #153 Black (K)
* 1 skein in #124 Barley (L)

For Golden Eggs

Vanna's Glamour® by Lion Brand® Yarn, 1¾oz/50g skeins, each approx 202yds/185m

* 1 skein in #186 Bronze (M)

THE HOOKS

For Jack and Beanstalk

Size G/6 (4mm) crochet hook

For Giant

Size K/10½ (6.5mm) crochet hook

For Golden Eggs

Size B/1 (2.25mm) crochet hook

THINGS FOR ALL

Polyfil Stuffing

Yarn Needle

2 black safety eyes 15mm for Giant

2 black safety eyes 8mm for Jack

MEASUREMENTS

Jack 5"/12.5cm tall

Giant 9"/23cm tall excluding hair

Beanstalk 11½"/29.5cm tall including leaves and vines

Golden Eggs ¾"/2cm

GAUGE

Gauge is not critical.

GIANT

Head

With H and K/10½ hook, ch 3, join with sl st to form ring.

Rnd 1: Ch 1, 6 sc in ring, sl st in beg ch.

Inc rnd 2: Ch 1, 2 sc in each st around, sl st in first st of rnd—12 sc.

Inc rnd 3: Ch 1, *2 sc in first st, sc in next st; rep from * around, sl st in first st of rnd—18 sts.

Inc rnd 4: Ch 1, *2 sc in first st, sc in next 2 sts; rep from * around, sl st in first st of rnd—24 sc.

Inc rnd 5: Ch 1, *2 sc in first st, sc in next 3 sts; rep from * around, sl st in first st of rnd—30 sc.

Rnds 6–11: Ch 1, sc in each st around, sl st in first st of rnd.

Place safety eyes between rnds 7 and 8, 4 sts apart.

Dec rnd 12: Ch 1, *sc2tog, sc in next 3 sts; rep from * around, sl st in first st of rnd—24 sc.

Dec rnd 13: Ch 1, *sc2tog, sc in next 2 sts; rep from * around, sl st in first st of rnd—18 sc.

Dec rnd 14: Ch 1, *sc2tog, sc in next st; rep from * around, sl st in first st of rnd—12 sc.

Stuff with polyfil.

Inc rnd 15: Ch 1, *2 sc in first st, sc in next 2 sts; rep from * around, sl st in first st of rnd—16 sc.

Body

Switch to I.

Inc rnd 16: Ch 1, *2 sc in first st, sc in next 3 sts; rep from * around, sl st in first st of rnd—20 sc.

Inc rnd 17: Ch 1, *2 sc in first st, sc in next 4 sts; rep from * around, sl st in first st of rnd—24 sc.

Rnds 18–21: Ch 1, sc in each st around, sl st in first st of rnd.

Switch to J.

Rnd 22: Ch 1, sc in each st around, sl st in first st of rnd.

Dec rnd 23: Ch 1, *sc2tog, sc in next 2 sts; rep from * around, sl st in first st of rnd—18 sc.

Dec rnd 24: Ch 1, *sc2tog, sc in next st; rep from * around, sl st in first st of rnd—12 sc.

Stuff with polyfil.

Dec rnd 25: Ch 1, sc2tog around, sl st in first st of rnd—6 sc.

Fasten off, leaving long tail. Thread tail through yarn needle, and weave around rem small opening. Pull tight to cinch closed.

Arms (make 2)

With H, ch 3, join with sl st to form ring.

Rnd 1: Ch 1, 6 sc in ring, sl st in beg ch.

Inc rnd 2: Ch 1, 2 sc in each st around, sl st in first st of rnd—12 sc.

Rnd 3: Ch 1, sc in each st around, sl st in first st of rnd.

Switch to I.

Rnd 4: Ch 1, sc in each st around, sl st in first st of rnd.

Dec rnd 5: Ch 1, sc2tog, sc around, sl st in first st of rnd—11 sc.

Dec rnd 6 Ch 1, sc2tog, sc around, sl st in first st of rnd—10 sc.

Dec rnd 7 Ch 1, sc2tog, sc around, sl st in first st of rnd—9 sc.

Dec rnd 8 Ch 1, sc2tog, sc around, sl st in first st of rnd—8 sc.

Rnd 9 (arm cap): Ch 1, [sl st in next st] twice, sc in next st, [dc in next st] twice, sc in next st, [sl st in next st] twice, sl st in first st of rnd. Fasten off.

Legs (make 2)

With K, ch 3, join with sl st to form ring.

Rnd 1: Ch 1, 6 sc in ring, sl st in beg ch.

Inc rnd 2: Ch 1, 2 sc in each st around, sl st in

first st of rnd—12 sc.

Rnd 3: Ch 1, sc in each st around, sl st in first st of rnd.

Switch to J.

Rnds 4 and 5: Ch 1, sc in each st around, sl st in first st of rnd.

Fasten off.

Collar (make 2)

With I, ch 10, sl st in 2nd st from hook, and in next 6 chs, sc in next ch, dc in next ch. Fasten off.

Finishing Giant

Stuff Arms and Legs with small amounts of polyfil. Stuff yarn ends into limbs instead of clipping or weaving in to help fill in limbs and use less stuffing. Leave about top third of Arms unstuffed so they lie closer to body. Sew Arms to either side of Body with tall side of Arm Cap at top next to neck. Sew Legs to Body; do not pinch opening closed—sew around edge keeping circular shape intact.

With K and yarn needle, make 3 french knot buttons down center front of shirt. Using photo as a guide, stitch plaid lines onto shirt, using the sc sts and rows as guides for making lines. Do not work across buttons. Sew eyebrows over safety eyes using yarn needle.

Sew Collar pieces onto shirt with dc stitches in front of shirt on either side of buttons. One collar piece will be sewn on with the WS facing.

Hair

With L, cut least 30 strands 8″/20.5cm lon for hair and 20 strands 5″/13cm long for beard and mustache. Attach as fringe to head and face. Trim fringe shorter for beard; trim fringe even shorter for mustache.

JACK

Head

With A, ch 3, join with sl st to form ring.

Rnd 1: Ch 1, sc 6 into ring, sl st in beg ch.

Inc rnd 2: Ch 1, 2 sc in each st around, sl st in first st of rnd—12 sc.

Inc rnd 3: Ch 1, *2 sc in first st, sc in next st; rep from * around, sl st in first st of rnd—18 sc.

Inc rnd 4: Ch 1, *2 sc in first st, sc in next 2 sts; rep from * around, sl st in first st of rnd—24 sc.

Inc rnd 5: Ch 1, *2 sc in first st, sc in next 3 sts; rep from * around, sl st in first st of rnd—30 sc.

Rnds 6–11: Ch 1, sc in each st around, sl st in first st of rnd.

Place safety eyes for Jack between rnds 7 and 8, 4 sts apart.

Dec rnd 12: Ch 1, *sc2tog, sc in next 3 sts; rep from * around, sl st in first st of rnd—24 sc.

Dec rnd 13: Ch 1, *sc2tog, sc in next 2 sts; rep from * around, sl st in first st of rnd—18 sc.

Dec rnd 14: Ch 1, *sc2tog, sc in next st; rep from * around, sl st in first st of rnd—12 sc.

Stuff with polyfil.

Inc rnd 15: Ch 1, *2 sc in first st, sc in next 2 sts; rep from * around, sl st in first st of rnd—16 sc.

Body

Switch to B.

Inc rnd 16: Ch 1, *2 sc in first st, sc in next 3 sts; rep from * around, sl st in first st of rnd—20 sc.

Inc rnd 17: Ch 1, *2 sc in first st, sc in next 4 sts; rep from * around, sl st in first st of rnd—24 sc.

Rnds 18–21: Ch 1, sc in each st around, sl st in first st of rnd.

Switch to C.

Rnd 22: Ch 1, sc in each st around, sl st in first st of rnd.

Dec rnd 23: Ch 1, *sc2tog, sc in next 2 sts; rep from * around, sl st in first st of rnd—18 sc.

Dec rnd 24: Ch 1, *sc2tog, sc in next st; rep from * around, sl st in first st of rnd—12 sc.

Stuff with polyfil.

Dec rnd 25: Ch 1, sc2tog around, sl st in first st of rnd—6 sc.

Fasten off, leaving long tail. Thread tail through yarn needle, and weave around rem small opening. Pull tight to cinch closed.

Arms (make 2)

With A, ch 3, join with sl st to form ring.

Rnd 1: Ch 1, sc 6 into ring, sl st in beg ch.

Inc rnd 2: Ch 1, 2 sc in each st around, sl st in first st of rnd—12 sc.

Rnd 3: Ch 1, sc in each st around, sl st in first st of rnd.

Switch to B.

Rnd 4: Ch 1, sc in each st around, sl st in first st of rnd.

Dec rnd 5: Ch 1, sc2tog, sc around, sl st in first st of rnd—11 sc.

Dec rnd 6: Ch 1, sc2tog, sc around, sl st in first st of rnd—10 sc.

Dec rnd 7: Ch 1, sc2tog, sc around, sl st in first st of rnd—9 sc.

Dec rnd 8: Ch 1, sc2tog, sc around, sl st in first st of rnd—8 sc.

Rnd 9 (arm cap): Ch 1, [sl st in next st] twice, sc in next st, [dc in next st] twice, sc in next st, [sl st in next st] twice, sl st in first st of rnd.

Fasten off.

Legs (make 2)

With D, ch 3, join with sl st to form ring.

Rnd 1: Ch 1, sc 6 into ring, sl st in beg ch.

Inc rnd 2: Ch 1, 2 sc in each st around, sl st in first st of rnd—12 sc.

Rnd 3: Ch 1, sc in each st around, sl st in first st of rnd.

Switch to C.

Rnds 4 and 5: Ch 1, sc in each st around, sl st in first st of rnd.

Fasten off.

Vest

With A, ch 26.

Row 1 (RS): Dc in second ch from hook and in each ch across—24 dc.

Dec row 2 (WS): Ch 2, turn, dc2tog, dc in next st, ch 3 and sk next 3 sts, dc in next 2 sts, dc2tog, dc in next 4 sts, dc2tog, dc in next 2 sts, ch 3 and sk next 3 sts, dc in next st, dc2tog—14 dc, 6 ch.

Row 3: Ch 1, turn, hdc in next 2 sts, 3 sc in ch-3 sp, hdc in next 10 sts, 3 sc in ch-3 sp, hdc in next 2 sts. Fasten off and weave in ends.

Finishing Jack

Stuff Arms and Legs with small amounts of polyfil. Stuff yarn ends into limbs instead of clipping or weaving in to help fill in limbs and use less stuffing. Leave about top third of Arms unstuffed so they lie closer to body. Sew Arms to either side of Body with tall side of Arm Cap at top next to neck. Sew Legs to Body; do not pinch opening closed—sew around edge, keeping circular shape intact.

Hair

Cut long strand of D. Using photo as a guide, sew hair onto top of head with long stitches. Start at bottom back of head and work way up, eventually making long stitches across top of head to form side part.

GOLDEN EGGS

(make 3)

With M, ch 3, join with sl st to form ring.

Rnd 1: Ch 1, 6 sc in ring, sl st in beg ch.

Rnd 2: Ch 1, 2 sc in each st around, sl st in first st of rnd—12 sc.

Rnds 3 and 4: Ch 1, sc in each st around, sl st in first st of rnd.

Dec rnd 5: Ch 1, *sc2tog, sc in next 4 sts; rep from * around, sl st in first st of rnd—10 sc.

Dec rnd 6: Ch 1, *sc2tog, sc in next 3 sts; rep from * around, sl st in first st of rnd—8 sc.

Dec rnd 7: Ch 1, *sc2tog, sc in next 2 sts; rep from * around, sl st in first st of rnd—6 sts.

Fasten off and sew top closed.

BEANSTALK

With F, ch 3, join with sl st to form ring.

Rnd 1: Ch 1, 6 sc in ring, sl st in beg ch.

Inc rnd 2: Ch 1, 2 sc in each st around, sl st in first st of rnd—12 sc.

Inc rnd 3: Ch 1, *2 sc in first st, sc in next st; rep from * around, sl st in first st of rnd—18 sc.

Inc rnd 4: Ch 1, *2 sc in first st, sc in next 2 sts; rep from * around, sl st in first st of rnd—24 sc.

Inc rnd 5: Ch 1, *2 sc in first st, sc in next 3 sts; rep from * around, sl st in first st of rnd—30 sc.

Inc rnd 6: Ch 1, *2 sc in first st, sc in next 4 sts; rep from * around, sl st in first st of rnd—36 sc.

Inc rnd 7: Ch 1, *2 sc in first st, sc in next 5 sts; rep from * around, sl st in first st of rnd—42 sc.

Rnd 8: Ch 1, sc into next st, working into the back loop only. Continue to work around in this manner. Do not join at end of rnd; work around in spiral.

Continue to crochet in spiral until beanstalk measures 10"/25.5cm from beg, ending at middle back of piece, do not fasten off. Mark beg of rnd.

Bottom

Inc rnd 1: Ch 1, *2 sc in first st, sc in next 6 sts; rep from * around, sl st in first st of rnd—48 sc.

Rnd 2: Ch 1, sc in each st around, sl st in first st of rnd.

Inc rnd 3: Ch 1, *2 sc in first st, sc in next 7 sts; rep from * around, sl st in first st of rnd—54 sc.

Rnd 4: Ch 1, sc in each st around, sl st in first st of rnd.

Inc rnd 5: Ch 1, *2 sc in first st, sc in next 8 sts; rep from * around, sl st in first st of rnd—60 sc.

Fasten off.

Base

With F, ch 3, join with sl st to form ring.

Rnd 1: Ch 1, 6 sc in ring, sl st in beg ch.

Inc rnd 2: Ch 1, 2 sc in each st around, sl st in first st of rnd—12 sc.

Inc rnd 3: Ch 1, *2 sc in first st, sc in next st; rep from * around, sl st in first st of rnd—18 sc.

Inc rnd 4: Ch 1, *2 sc in first st, sc in next 2 sts; rep from * around, sl st in first st of rnd—24 sc.

Inc rnd 5: Ch 1, *2 sc in first st, sc in next 3 sts; rep from * around, sl st in first st of rnd—30 sc.

Inc rnd 6: Ch 1, *2 sc in first st, sc in next 4 sts; rep from * around, sl st in first st of rnd—36 sc.

Inc rnd 7: Ch 1, *2 sc in first st, sc in next 5 sts; rep from * around, sl st in first st of rnd—42 sc.

Inc rnd 8: Ch 1, *2 sc in first st, sc in next 6 sts; rep from * around, sl st in first st of rnd—48 sc.

Inc rnd 9: Ch 1, *2 sc in first st, sc in next 7 sts; rep from * around, sl st in first st of rnd—54 sc.

Inc rnd 10: Ch 1, *2 sc in first st, sc in next 8 sts; rep from * around, sl st in first st of rnd—60 sc.

Finishing Beanstalk

Take Beanstalk and Base, with wrong sides facing each other; place Beanstalk in front and Base in back; insert hook into one st and corresponding st on other piece, sc pieces tog. Start at beg/end of rnds, work around leaving small opening. Stuff Beanstalk with polyfil, continue sc around. Fasten off.

Note Don't overstuff bottom so that base doesn't curve outward. Bottom should lie flat.

Vines

Note Make 2, one each in B and G

Small Leaf

*Ch 5.

Row 1: Sl st in next ch, sc in next 2 ch, sl st in next ch. Turn.

Row 2: Ch 1, sl st in next st, sc in next 2 sts, sl st in next st.

Row 3: Ch 2, dc next to chs just made, work 3 dc down other side of beg ch-5, sl st into bottom of leaf.

Ch 8.

Large Leaf

Ch 9.

Row 1: Sl st in next ch, sc in next 6 ch, sl st in next ch. Turn.

Row 2: Ch 1, sl st in next st, sc in next 6 sts, sl st in next st.

Row 3: Ch 2, dc next to chs just made, work 7 dc down other side of beg ch-9, sl st into bottom of leaf.

Ch 8.

Rep from * until vine is long enough to wrap around Beanstalk.

Using photo on page 43 as a guide, wrap G Vine around Beanstalk and sew in place. Wrap B Vine around Beanstalk in opposite direction and sew in place.

Loose Leaves
Small (make 6)

With F, ch 5.

Row 1: Sl st in next ch, sc in next 2 ch, sl st in next ch. Turn.

Row 2: Ch 1, sl st in next st, sc in next 2 sts, sl st in next st.

Row 3: Ch 2, dc next to chs just made, work 3 dc down other side of beg ch-5, sl st into bottom of leaf.

Fasten off.

Large (make 2)

With F, ch 9.

Row 1: Sl st in next ch, sc in next 6 ch, sl st in next ch. Turn.

Row 2: Ch 1, sl st in next st, sc in next 6 sts, sl st in next st.

Row 3: Ch 2, dc next to chs just made, work 7 dc down other side of beg ch-9, sl st into bottom of leaf.

Fasten off.

Sew leaves onto Beanstalk.

Tom Thumb

A poor woodman sat in his cottage one night, smoking his pipe by the fireside, while his wife sat by his side spinning. "How lonely it is, wife," said he, as he puffed out a long curl of smoke, "for you and me to sit here by ourselves, without any children to play about and amuse us while other people seem so happy and merry with their children!" "What you say is very true," said the wife, sighing, and turning round her wheel; "how happy should I be if I had but one child! If it were ever so small—nay, if it were no bigger than my thumb—I should be very happy, and love it dearly." Now—odd as you may think it—it came to pass that this good woman's wish was fulfilled, just in the very way she had wished it; for, not long afterwards, she had a little boy, who was quite healthy and strong, but was not much bigger than my thumb. So they said, "Well, we cannot say we have not got what we wished for, and, little as he is, we will love him dearly." And they called him Thomas Thumb.

They gave him plenty of food, yet for all they could do he never grew bigger, but kept just the same size as he had been when he was born. Still, his eyes were sharp and sparkling, and he soon showed himself to be a clever little fellow, who always knew well what he was about.

One day, as the woodman was getting ready to go into the wood to cut fuel, he said, "I wish I had someone to bring the cart after me, for I want to make haste." "Oh, father," cried Tom, "I will take care of that; the cart shall be in the wood by the time you want it." Then the woodman laughed, and said, "How can that be? You cannot reach up to the horse's bridle." "Never mind that, father," said Tom; "if my mother will only harness the horse, I will get into his ear and tell him which way to go." "Well," said the father, "we will try for once."

When the time came the mother harnessed the horse to the cart, and put Tom into his ear; and as he sat there the little man told the beast how to go, crying out, "Go on!" and "Stop!" as he wanted: and thus the horse went on just as well as if the woodman had driven it himself into the wood. It happened that as the horse was going a little too fast, and Tom was calling out, "Gently! gently!" two strangers came up. "What an odd thing that is!" said one: "there is a cart going along, and I hear a carter talking to the horse, but yet I can see no one." "That is queer, indeed," said the other; "let us follow the cart, and see where it goes." So they went on into the wood, till at last they came to the place where the woodman was. Then Tom Thumb, seeing his father, cried out, "See, father, here I am with the cart, all right and safe! now take me down!" So his father took hold of the horse with one hand, and with the other took his son out of the horse's ear, and put him down upon a straw, where he sat as merry as you please.

The two strangers were all this time looking on, and did not know what to say for wonder. At last one took the other aside, and said, "That little urchin will make our fortune, if we can get him, and carry him about from town to town as a show; we must buy him." So they went up to the wood-man, and asked him what he would take for the little man. "He will be better off," said they, "with us than with you." "I won't sell him at all," said the father; "my own flesh and blood is dearer to me than all the silver and gold in the world." But Tom, hearing of the bargain they wanted to make, crept up his father's coat to his shoulder and whispered in his ear, "Take the money, father, and let them have me; I'll soon come back to you."

So the woodman at last said he would sell Tom to the strangers for a large piece of gold, and they paid the price. "Where would you like to sit?" said one of them. "Oh, put me on the rim of your hat; that will be a nice gallery for me; I can walk about there and see the country as we go along." So they did as he wished; and when Tom had taken leave of his father they took him away with them.

They journeyed on till it began to be dusky, and then the little man said, "Let me get down, I'm tired." So the man took off his hat, and put him down on a clod of earth, in a ploughed field by the side of the road. But Tom ran about amongst the furrows, and at last slipped into an old mouse-hole. "Good night, my masters!" said he, "I'm off! Mind and look sharp after me the next time." Then they ran at once to the place, and poked the ends of their sticks into the mouse-hole, but all in vain; Tom only crawled farther and farther in; and at last it became quite dark, so that they were forced to go their way without their prize, as sulky as could be.

When Tom found they were gone, he came out of his hiding-place. "What dangerous walking it is," said he, "in this ploughed field! If I were to fall from one of these great clods, I should undoubtedly break my neck." At last, by good luck, he found a large empty snail-shell. "This is lucky," said he, "I can sleep here very well"; and in he crept.

Just as he was falling asleep, he heard two men passing by, chatting together; and one said to the other, "How can we rob that rich parson's house of his silver and gold?" "I'll tell you!" cried Tom. "What noise was that?" said the thief, frightened; "I'm sure I heard someone speak." They stood still listening, and Tom said, "Take me with you, and I'll soon show you how to get the parson's money." "But where are you?" said they. "Look about on the ground," answered he, "and listen where the sound comes from." At last the thieves found him out, and lifted him up in their hands. "You little urchin!" they said, "what can you do for us?" "Why, I can get between the iron window-bars of the parson's house, and throw you out whatever you want." "That's a good thought," said the thieves; "come along, we shall see what you can do."

When they came to the parson's house, Tom slipped through the window bars into the room, and then called out as loud as he could bawl, "Will you have all that is here?" At this the thieves were frightened, and said, "Softly, softly! Speak low, that you may not awaken anybody." But Tom seemed as if he did not understand them, and bawled out again, "How much will you have? Shall I throw it all out?" Now the cook lay in the next room; and hearing a noise she raised herself up in her bed and listened. Meantime the thieves were frightened, and ran off a little way; but at last they plucked up their hearts, and said, "The little urchin is only trying to make fools of us." So they came back and whispered softly to him, saying, "Now let us have no more of your roguish jokes; but throw us out some of the money." Then Tom called out as loud as he could, "Very well! Hold your hands! Here it comes."

The cook heard this quite plain, so she sprang out of bed, and ran to open the door. The thieves ran off as if a wolf was at their tails: and the maid, having groped about and found nothing, went away for a light. By the time she came back, Tom had slipped off into the barn; and when she had looked about and searched every hole and corner, and found nobody, she went to bed, thinking she must have been dreaming with her eyes open.

The little man crawled about in the hay-loft, and at last found a snug place to finish his night's rest in; so he laid himself down, meaning to sleep till daylight, and then find his way home to his father and mother. But alas! How woefully he was undone! What crosses and sorrows happen to us all in this world! The cook got up early, before daybreak, to feed the cows; and going straight to the hay-loft, carried away a large bundle of hay, with the little man in the middle of it, fast asleep. He still, however, slept on, and did not awake till he found himself in the mouth of the cow; for the cook had put the hay into the cow's rick, and the cow had taken Tom up in a mouthful of it. "Good lack-a-day!" said he, "how came I to tumble into the mill?" But he soon found out where he really was; and was forced to have all his wits about him, that he might not get between the cow's teeth, and so be crushed to death. At last down he went into her stomach. "It is rather dark," said he; "they forgot to build windows in this room to let the sun in; a candle would be no bad thing."

Though he made the best of his bad luck, he did not like his quarters at all; and the worst of it was, that more and more hay was always coming down, and the space left for him became smaller and smaller. At last he cried out as loud as he could, "Don't bring me any more hay! Don't bring me any more hay!"

The maid happened to be just then milking the cow; and hearing someone speak, but seeing nobody, and yet being quite sure it was the same voice that she had heard in the night, she was so frightened that she fell off her stool, and overset the milk-pail. As soon as she could pick herself up out of the dirt, she ran off as fast as she could to her master the parson, and said, "Sir, sir, the cow is talking!" But the parson said, "Woman, thou art surely mad!" However, he went with her into the cow-house, to try and see what was the matter.

Scarcely had they set foot on the threshold, when Tom called out, "Don't bring me any more hay!" Then the parson himself was frightened; and thinking the cow was surely bewitched, told his man to kill her on the spot. So the cow was killed, and cut up; and the stomach, in which Tom lay, was thrown out upon a dunghill.

Tom soon set himself to work to get out, which was not a very easy task; but at last, just as he had made room to get his head out, fresh ill-luck befell him. A hungry wolf sprang out, and swallowed up the whole stomach, with Tom in it, at one gulp, and ran away.

Tom, however, was still not disheartened; and thinking the wolf would not dislike having some chat with him as he was going along, he called out, "My good friend, I can show you a famous treat." "Where's that?" said the wolf. "In such and such a house," said Tom, describing his own father's house. "You can crawl through the drain into the kitchen and then into the pantry, and there you will find cakes, ham, beef, cold chicken, roast pig, apple-dumplings, and everything that your heart can wish."

The wolf did not want to be asked twice; so that very night he went to the house and crawled through the drain into the kitchen, and then into the pantry, and ate and drank there to his heart's content. As soon as he had had enough he wanted to get away; but he had eaten so much that he could not go out by the same way he came in.

This was just what Tom had reckoned upon; and now he began to set up a great shout, making all the noise he could. "Will you be easy?" said the wolf; "you'll awaken everybody in the house if you make such a clatter." "What's that to me?" said the little man; "you have had your frolic, now I've a mind to be merry myself"; and he began, singing and shouting as loud as he could.

The woodman and his wife, being awakened by the noise, peeped through a crack in the door; but when they saw a wolf was there, you may well suppose that they were sadly frightened; and the woodman ran for his axe, and gave his wife a scythe. "Do you stay behind," said the woodman, "and when I have knocked him on the head you must rip him up with the scythe." Tom heard all this, and cried out, "Father, father! I am here, the wolf has swallowed me." And his father said, "Heaven be praised! We have found our dear child again"; and he told his wife not to use the scythe for fear she should hurt him. Then he aimed a great blow, and struck the wolf on the head, and killed him on the spot! And when he was dead they cut open his body, and set Tommy free. "Ah!" said the father, "what fears we have had for you!" "Yes, father," answered he; "I have travelled all over the world, I think, in one way or other, since we parted; and now I am very glad to come home and get fresh air again." "Why, where have you been?" said his father. "I have been in a mouse-hole—and in a snail-shell—and down a cow's throat—and in the wolf's belly; and yet here I am again, safe and sound."

"Well," said they, "you are come back, and we will not sell you again for all the riches in the world."

Then they hugged and kissed their dear little son, and gave him plenty to eat and drink, for he was very hungry; and then they fetched new clothes for him, for his old ones had been quite spoiled on his journey. So Master Thumb stayed at home with his father and mother, in peace; for though he had been so great a traveller, and had done and seen so many fine things, and was fond enough of telling the whole story, he always agreed that, after all, there's no place like HOME!

Tom Thumb

SKILL LEVEL
Easy

Things you'll need:

THE YARN

For Cow

Classic Wool Worsted™ by Patons®, 3½oz/100g skeins, each approx 192yds/210m

* 1 skein in #00202 Aran (A)
* 1 skein in #00226 Black (B)
* 1 skein in #77615 Yellow (C)

For Tom Thumb

Kroy Socks by Patons®, 1¾oz/50g skeins, each approx. 166yds/152m

* 1 skein in #008 Muslin (D)
* 1 skein in #705 Red (E)
* 1 skein in #011 Flax (F)
* 1 skein in #042 Gentry Grey (G)

THE HOOKS

For Cow

Size G/6 (4mm) crochet hook

For Tom Thumb

Size B/1 (2.25mm) crochet hook

THINGS FOR ALL

Polyfil Stuffing

Yarn Needle

2 black safety eyes 15mm for Giant

2 black safety eyes 8mm for Jack

MEASUREMENTS

Cow 5¼"/13.5cm tall including ears and horns

Tom Thumb 2¼"/5.5cm tall including legs and hat

GAUGE

Gauge is not critical.

COW

Body

With A and G/6 hook, ch 3, join with sl st to form ring.

Rnd 1: Ch 1, 6 sc in ring, sl st in beg ch.

Inc rnd 2: Ch 1, 2 sc in each st around, sl st in first st of rnd—12 sc.

Inc rnd 3: Ch 1, *2 sc in first st, sc in next st; rep from * around, sl st in first st of rnd—18 sc.

Inc rnd 4: Ch 1, *2 sc in first st, sc in next 2 sts; rep from * around, sl st in first st of rnd—24 sc.

Inc rnd 5: Ch 1, *2 sc in first st, sc in next 3 sts; rep from * around, sl st in first st of rnd—30 sc.

Rnds 6–22: Ch 1, sc in each st around, sl st in first st of rnd.

Dec rnd 23: Ch 1, *sc2tog, sc in next 3 sts; rep from * around, sl st in first st of rnd—24 sc.

Dec rnd 24: Ch 1, *sc2tog, sc in next 2 sts; rep from * around, sl st in first st of rnd—18 sc.

Stuff with polyfil.

Dec rnd 25: Ch 1, *sc2tog, sc in next st; rep from * around, sl st in first st of rnd—12 sc.

Dec rnd 26: Ch 1, sc2tog around, sl st in first st of rnd—6 sc.

Fasten off, leaving long tail. Thread tail through yarn needle, weave around rem small opening. Pull tight to cinch closed.

Head

With A, ch 3, join with sl st to form ring.

Rnd 1: Ch 1, 6 sc in ring, sl st in beg ch.

Inc rnd 2: Ch 1, 2 sc in each st around, sl st in first st of rnd—12 sc.

Inc rnd 3: Ch 1, *2 sc in first st, sc in next st; rep from * around, sl st in first st of rnd—18 sc.

Inc rnd 4: Ch 1, *2 sc in first st, sc in next 2 sts; rep from * around, sl st in first st of rnd—24 sc.

Inc rnd 5: Ch 1, *2 sc in first st, sc in next 3 sts; rep from * around, sl st in first st of rnd—30 sc.

Rnds 6–11: Ch 1, sc in each st around, sl st in first st of rnd.

Place safety eyes between rnds 7 and 8, 4 sts apart

Dec rnd 12: Ch 1, *sc2tog, sc in next 3 sts; rep from * around, sl st in first st of rnd—24 sc.

Dec rnd 13: Ch 1, *sc2tog, sc in next 2 sts; rep from * around, sl st in first st of rnd—18 sc.

Dec rnd 14: Ch 1, *sc2tog, sc in next st; rep from * around, sl st in first st of rnd—12 sc.

Stuff head with polyfil.

Dec rnd 15: Ch 1, sc2tog around, sl st in first st of rnd—6 sc.

Fasten off, leaving long tail. Thread tail through yarn needle, and weave around rem small opening. Pull tight to cinch closed.

Snout

With A, ch 5, *2 sc in first ch, sc in next 3 chs, 2 sc in last ch; rep from * once more on opposite side of ch, join with sl st in first st—14 sc.

Inc rnd 2: Ch 1, *sc in next st, 2 sc in next st, sc in next 3 sts, 2 sc in next st, sc in next st; rep from * once more, sl st in first st of rnd—18 sc.

Rnds 3–4: Ch 1, sc in each st around, sl st in first st of rnd.

Fasten off.

Ears (make 2; 1 with A and 1 with B)

Ch 3, join with sl st to form ring.

Rnd 1: Ch 1, 6 sc in ring, sl st in beg ch.

Rnd 2: Ch 1, sc in each st around, sl st in first st of rnd.

Inc rnd 3: Ch 1, *2 sc in next st, sc in next st; rep from * around—9 sc.

Rnd 4: Ch 1, sc in each st around, sl st in first st of rnd.

Dec rnd 5: Ch 1, *sc2tog, sc in next st; rep from * around—6 sc.

Fasten off.

Horns (make 2)

With C, ch 3, join with sl st to form ring.

Rnd 1: Ch 1, 6 sc in ring, sl st in beg ch.

Rnd 2: Ch 1, sc in each st around, sl st in first st of rnd.

Fasten off.

Legs (make 4; 2 with A, and 2 with B for rnds 1 and 2, A for rem)

With A, ch 3, join with sl st to form ring.

Rnd 1: Ch 1, 6 sc in ring, sl st in beg ch.

Inc rnd 2: Ch 1, 2 sc in each st around, sl st in first st of rnd—12 sc.

Rnds 3–5: Ch 1, sc in each st around, sl st in first st of rnd.

Fasten off.

Spots

Large Spots (make 4)

With B, ch 3, join with sl st to form ring.

Rnd 1: Ch 1, 6 sc in ring, sl st in beg ch.

Inc rnd 2: Ch 1, 2 sc in each st around, sl st in first st of rnd—12 sc.

Fasten off.

Small Spots (make 3)

With B, ch 3, join with sl st to form ring.

Rnd 1: Ch 1, 6 sc in ring, sl st in beg ch.

Fasten off.

Finishing Cow

Using photo on page 53 as a guide, sew Snout to front of Head. With B and yarn needle, make 2 vertical straight sts for nostrils. Sew Horns to top of Head, and sew Ears to upper sides of Head.

Sew Legs to Body; do not pinch opening closed —sew around edge to keep circular shape intact. Sew Head to Body.

Note Since Head is large compared to Body, check balance of Head on Body by stitching on with temporary stitches that can be pulled out if needed. When balance of Head on Body works, secure stitches.

Sew spots to body randomly, but place one large spot on back of head.

Tail

With A, cut 3 long strands. Using photo as guide, with yarn needle, thread all 3 strands tog at bottom of cow. Braid strands tog, to desired length. With C, tie bow around bottom of braid. Trim ends of braid.

TOM THUMB

Head

With D and B/1 hook, ch 3, join with sl st to form ring.

Rnd 1: Ch 1, sc 6 in ring, sl st in beg ch.

Inc rnd 2: Ch 1, *2 sc in next st, sc in next 2 sts; rep from * around—8 sc.

Rnds 3 and 4: Ch 1, sc in each st around, sl st in first st of rnd.

Dec rnd 5: Ch 1, sc2tog around—4 sc.

Body

Switch to E.

Inc rnd 6: Ch 1, 2 sc in each st around—8 sc.

Rnds 7 and 8: Ch 1, sc in each st around, sl st in first st of rnd.

Switch to F.

Rnd 9: Ch 1, sc in each st around, sl st in first st of rnd.

Dec rnd 10: Ch 1, sc2tog around—4 sc.

Fasten off, leaving long tail. Thread tail through yarn needle, and weave around rem small opening. Pull tight to cinch closed.

Arms/Legs (make 2; 1 in E for Arms, 1 in F for Legs)

Ch 12. Fasten off. Weave in ends by working back and forth through back of ch before cutting yarn.

Hat

With F, ch 3, join with sl st to form ring.

Rnd 1: Ch 1, sc 6 in ring, sl st in beg ch.

Rnd 2: Ch 1, sc in each st around, sl st in first st of rnd.

Inc rnd 3: Ch 1, 2 sc in each st around, sl st in first st of rnd—12 sc.

Fasten off.

Finishing Tom Thumb

Hair

With G, cut long strand. Using photo on page 55 as a guide and yarn needle, sew hair on top of head using long sts. Start at bottom back of head and work way up, eventually making long stitches across top of head to form side part.

Tack Hat on top of head.

Thread Arm ch onto yarn needle, and insert needle into one side of Body and out other. Center Arms between Body, no need to stitch into place. Rep with Leg ch on bottom of Body.

Rapunzel

Rapunzel

There were once a man and a woman who had long in vain wished for a child. At length the woman hoped that God was about to grant her desire. These people had a little window at the back of their house from which a splendid garden could be seen, which was full of the most beautiful flowers and herbs. It was, however, surrounded by a high wall, and no one dared to go into it because it belonged to an enchantress, who had great power and was dreaded by all the world. One day the woman was standing by this window and looking down into the garden, when she saw a bed which was planted with the most beautiful rampion (rapunzel), and it looked so fresh and green that she longed for it, she quite pined away, and began to look pale and miserable. Then her husband was alarmed, and asked: "What ails you, dear wife?" "Ah," she replied, "if I can't eat some of the rampion, which is in the garden behind our house, I shall die." The man, who loved her, thought: "Sooner than let your wife die, bring her some of the rampion yourself, let it cost what it will." At twilight, he clambered down over the wall into the garden of the enchantress, hastily clutched a handful of rampion, and took it to his wife. She at once made herself a salad of it, and ate it greedily. It tasted so good to her—so very good, that the next day she longed for it three times as much as before.

If he was to have any rest, her husband must once more descend into the garden. In the gloom of evening therefore, he let himself down again; but when he had clambered down the wall he was terribly afraid, for he saw the enchantress standing before him. "How can you dare," said she with angry look, "descend into my garden and steal my rampion like a thief? You shall suffer for it!" "Ah," answered he, "let mercy take the place of justice, I only made up my mind to do it out of necessity. My wife saw your rampion from the window, and felt such a longing for it that she would have died if she had not got some to eat." Then the enchantress allowed her anger to be softened, and said to him: "If the case be as you say, I will allow you to take away with you as much rampion as you will, only I make one condition, you must give me the child which your wife will bring into the world; it shall be well treated, and I will care for it like a mother." The man in his terror consented to everything, and when the woman was brought to bed, the enchantress appeared at once, gave the child the name of Rapunzel, and took it away with her.

Rapunzel grew into the most beautiful child under the sun. When she was twelve years old, the enchantress shut her into a tower, which lay in a forest, and had neither stairs nor door, but quite at the top was a little window. When the enchantress wanted to go in, she placed herself beneath it and cried:

> *"Rapunzel, Rapunzel,*
> *Let down your hair to me."*

Rapunzel had magnificent long hair, fine as spun gold, and when she heard the voice of the enchantress she unfastened her braided tresses, wound them round one of the hooks of the window above, and then the hair fell twenty ells down, and the enchantress climbed up by it.

After a year or two, it came to pass that the king's son rode through the forest and passed by the tower. Then he heard a song, which was so charming that he stood still and listened. This was Rapunzel, who in her solitude passed her time in letting her sweet voice resound. The king's son wanted to climb up to her, and looked for the door of the tower, but none was to be found. He rode home, but the singing had so deeply touched his heart, that every day he went out into the forest and listened to it. Once when he was thus standing behind a tree, he saw that an enchantress came there, and he heard how she cried:

"Rapunzel, Rapunzel,
Let down your hair to me."

Then Rapunzel let down the braids of her hair, and the enchantress climbed up to her. "If that is the ladder by which one mounts, I too will try my fortune," said he, and the next day when it began to grow dark, he went to the tower and cried:

"Rapunzel, Rapunzel,
Let down your hair to me."

Immediately the hair fell down and the king's son climbed up.

At first Rapunzel was terribly frightened when a man, such as her eyes had never yet beheld, came to her; but the king's son began to talk to her quite like a friend, and told her that his heart had been so stirred that it had let him have no rest, and he had been forced to see her. Then Rapunzel lost her fear, and when he asked her if she would take him for her husband, and she saw that he was young and handsome, she thought: "He will love me more than old Dame Gothel does"; and she said yes, and laid her hand in his. She said: "I will willingly go away with you, but I do not know how to get down. Bring with you a skein of silk every time that you come, and I will weave a ladder with it, and when that is ready I will descend, and you will take me on your horse." They agreed that until that time he should come to her every evening, for the old woman came by day. The enchantress remarked nothing of this, until once Rapunzel said to her: "Tell me, Dame Gothel, how it happens that you are so much heavier for me to draw up than the young king's son—he is with me in a moment." "Ah! you wicked child," cried the enchantress. "What do I hear you say! I thought I had separated you from all the world, and yet you have deceived me!" In her anger she clutched Rapunzel's beautiful tresses, wrapped them twice round her left hand, seized a pair of scissors with the right, and snip, snap, they were cut off, and the lovely braids lay on the ground. And she was so pitiless that she took poor Rapunzel into a desert where she had to live in great grief and misery.

On the same day that she cast out Rapunzel, however, the enchantress fastened the braids of hair, which she had cut off, to the hook of the window, and when the king's son came and cried:

> *"Rapunzel, Rapunzel,*
> *Let down your hair to me."*

She let her hair down. The king's son ascended, but instead of finding his dearest Rapunzel, he found the enchantress, who gazed at him with wicked and venomous looks. "Aha!" she cried mockingly, "you would fetch your dearest, but the beautiful bird sits no longer singing in the nest; the cat has got it, and will scratch out your eyes as well. Rapunzel is lost to you; you will never see her again." The king's son was beside himself with pain, and in his despair he leapt down from the tower. He escaped with his life, but the thorns into which he fell pierced his eyes. Then he wandered quite blind about the forest, ate nothing but roots and berries, and did naught but lament and weep over the loss of his dearest wife. Thus he roamed about in misery for some years, and at length came to the desert where Rapunzel, with the twins to which she had given birth, a boy and a girl, lived in wretchedness. He heard a voice, and it seemed so familiar to him that he went towards it, and when he approached, Rapunzel knew him and fell on his neck and wept. Two of her tears wetted his eyes and they grew clear again, and he could see with them as before. He led her to his kingdom where he was joyfully received, and they lived for a long time afterwards, happy and contented.

Rapunzel

Things you'll need:

THE YARN

Deborah Norville Collection Everyday® Soft Worsted Solids by Premier® Yarns, 4oz/113g skeins, each approx 203yds/186m

* 1 skein in #1035 Cappucino (A)
* 1 skein in #1032 Peony (B)
* 1 skein in #1021 Magenta (C)
* 1 skein in #1001 Snow White (D)
* 1 skein in #1017 Azure (E)
* 1 skein in #1009 Royal Blue (F)
* 1 skein in #1024 Steel (G)
* 1 skein in #1011 Chocolate (H)
* 1 skein in #1003 Baby Yellow (I)

For Rapunzel

Starbella® Flash™ by Premier® Yarns, 3½oz/100g skeins, each approx 33yds/30m

* 1 skein in #1607 Pink Topaz (J)

Flowers by Premier® Yarns, 3½oz/100g skeins, each approx 108yds/99m

* 1 skein in #0028 Spring Bouquet (K)

For Tower

Mega™ Tweed by Premier® Yarns, 6oz/170g skeins, each approx 74yds/68m

* 1 skein in #0002 Gray Tweed (L)
* 1 skein in #0004 Brown Tweed (M)

THE HOOKS

Size G/6 (4mm) crochet hook

Size N/15 (10mm) crochet hook

THINGS FOR ALL

Polyfil Stuffing

Yarn Needle

4 black safety eyes 8mm for Rapunzel and Prince

MEASUREMENTS

Rapunzel 5¼"/13.5cm tall excluding hair
Prince 4½"/11.5cm tall excluding hair and crown
Tower 19¾"/50cm tall

GAUGE

Gauge is not critical.

RAPUNZEL

Head

With A and smaller hook, ch 3, join with sl st to form ring.

Rnd 1: Ch 1, sc 6 in ring, sl st in beg ch.

Inc rnd 2: Ch 1, 2 sc in each st around, sl st in first st of rnd—12 sc.

Inc rnd 3: Ch 1, *2 sc in first st, sc in next st; rep from * around, sl st in first st of rnd—18 sc.

Inc rnd 4: Ch 1, *2 sc in first st, sc in next 2 sts; rep from * around, sl st in first st of rnd—24 sc.

Inc rnd 5: Ch 1, *2 sc in first st, sc in next 3 sts; rep from * around, sl st in first st of rnd—30 sc.

Rnds 6–11: Ch 1, sc in each st around, sl st in first st of rnd.

Place safety eyes between rnds 7 and 8, 4 sts apart.

Dec rnd 12: Ch 1, *sc2tog, sc in next 3 sts; rep from * around, sl st in first st of rnd—24 sc.

Dec rnd 13: Ch 1, *sc2tog, sc in next 2 sts; rep from * around, sl st in first st of rnd—18 sc.

Dec rnd 14: Ch 1, *sc2tog, sc in next st; rep from * around, sl st in first st of rnd—12 sc.

Stuff with polyfil.

Inc rnd 15: Ch 1, *2 sc in first st, sc in next 2 sts; rep from * around, sl st in first st of rnd—16 sc.

Body

Switch to B.

Inc rnd 16: Ch 1, *2 sc in first st, sc in next 3 sts; rep from * around, sl st in first st of rnd—20 sc.

Inc rnd 17: Ch 1, *2 sc in first st, sc in next 4 sts; rep from * around, sl st in first st of rnd—24 sc.

Rnds 18–24: Ch 1, sc in each st around, sl st in first st of rnd.

Switch to C.

Rnd 25: Ch 1, sc in each st around. Sl st in first st of rnd.

Inc rnd 26: Ch 1, *2 sc in first st, sc in next 3 sts; rep from * around, sl st in first st of rnd—30 sc.

Rnd 27: Ch 1, sc in each st around, sl st in first st of rnd.

Inc rnd 28: Ch 1, *2 sc in first st, sc in next 4 sts; rep from * around, sl st in first st of rnd—36 sc.

Rnd 29: Ch 1, sc in each st around, sl st in first st of rnd.

Inc rnd 30: Ch 1, *2 sc in first st, sc in next 3 sts; rep from * around, sl st in first st of rnd—45 sc.

Fasten off.

Base

With C, ch 3, join with sl st to form ring.

Rnd 1: Ch 1, 6 sc in ring, sl st in beg ch.

Inc rnd 2: Ch 1, 2 sc in each st around, sl st in first st of rnd—12 sc.

Inc rnd 3: Ch 1, *2 sc in first st, sc in next st; rep from * around, sl st in first st of rnd—18 sts.

Inc rnd 4: Ch 1, *2 sc in first st, sc in next 2 sts; rep from * around, sl st in first st of rnd—24 sts.

Inc rnd 5: Ch 1, *2 sc in first st, sc in next 3 sts; rep from * around, sl st in first st of rnd—30 sc.

Inc rnd 6: Ch 1, *2 sc in first st, sc in next 4 sts; rep from * around, sl st in first st of rnd—36 sc.

Inc rnd 7: Ch 1, *2 sc in first st, sc in next 3 sts; rep from * around, sl st in first st of rnd—45 sc.

Fasten off.

Arms (make 2)

With A, ch 3, join with sl st to form ring.

Rnd 1: Ch 1, 6 sc in ring, sl st in beg ch.

Inc rnd 2: Ch 1, 2 sc in each st around, sl st in first st of rnd—12 sts.

Rnd 3: Ch 1, sc in each st around, sl st in first st of rnd.

Switch to B.

Rnd 4: Ch 1, sc in each st around, sl st in first st of rnd.

Dec rnd 5: Ch 1, sc2tog, sc around, sl st in first st of rnd—11 sc.

Dec rnd 6: Ch 1, sc2tog, sc around, sl st in first st of rnd—10 sc.

Dec rnd 7: Ch 1, sc2tog, sc around, sl st in first st of rnd—9 sc.

Dec rnd 8: Ch 1, sc2tog, sc around, sl st in first st of rnd—8 sc.

Rnd 9 (arm cap): Ch 1, [sl st in next st] twice, sc in next st, [dc in next st] twice, sc in next st, [sl st in next st] twice, sl st in first st of rnd.

Fasten off.

Finishing Rapunzel

Take Rapunzel and Base, and, with wrong sides facing each other, place Rapunzel in front and Base in back; insert hook into one st and corresponding st on other piece, sc pieces tog. Start at beg/end of rnds, work around leaving small opening. Stuff Body with polyfil, continue sc around. Fasten off.

Note Don't overstuff bottom so that base doesn't curve outward. Bottom should lie flat.

Ruffle Skirt

Note Unfold J as you work, and work into top line of spaces in ruffle, on opposite edge of metallic.

With smaller hook, insert hook into first complete space from front to back. Insert hook into second space and draw through first space. *Insert hook through next space and draw through loop on hook; rep from * until ch measures about 13"/33cm, slightly stretched. Starting at middle back, 2 rnds below color change, sew around ruffle around Body. Move ruffle up to just above color change and ending at middle back. Fasten end through live st. Tack edges of ruffle yarn onto back of dress if desired.

Sash

With C, ch 50. Fasten off. Weave in ends by working back and forth through back of ch before cutting yarn. Tie ch in bow around waist, on top of where ruffle skirt edge lies.

Stuff Arms with small amounts of polyfil. Stuff yarn ends into Arms instead of cutting or weaving in, to help fill in Arms and use less stuffing. Leave about top third of Arms unstuffed so they lie closer to Body. Sew Arms to either side of Body with tall side of Arm Cap at top next to neck.

Rapunzel Hair

With K, cut 15 strands each at least 40"/101.5cm long. With yarn needle and using photo as guide, attach as fringe to head down center part and down back of head. Make long braid. With B, tie a bow at end of braid. Trim ends of braid.

PRINCE

Head

With A and smaller hook, ch 3, join with sl st to form ring.

Rnd 1: Ch 1, sc 6 in ring, sl st in beg ch.

Inc rnd 2: Ch 1, 2 sc in each st around, sl st in first st of rnd—12 sc.

Inc rnd 3: Ch 1, *2 sc in first st, sc in next st; rep from * around, sl st in first st of rnd—18 sc.

Inc rnd 4: Ch 1, *2 sc in first st, sc in next 2 sts; rep from * around, sl st in first st of rnd—24 sc.

Inc rnd 5: Ch 1, *2 sc in first st, sc in next 3 sts; rep from * around, sl st in first st of rnd—30 sc.

Rnds 6–12: Ch 1, sc in each st around, sl st in first st of rnd.

Place safety eyes between rnds 7 and 8, 4 sts apart.

Rnd 23: Ch 1, sc in each st around, sl st in first st of rnd.

Dec rnd 24: Ch 1, *sc2tog, sc in next 2 sts; rep from * around, sl st in first st of rnd—18 sc.

Dec rnd 25: Ch 1, *sc2tog, sc in next st; rep from * around, sl st in first st of rnd—12 sc.

Stuff with polyfill.

Dec rnd 26: Ch 1, sc2tog around, sl st in first st of rnd—6 sc.

Fasten off, leaving long tail. Thread tail through yarn needle, and weave around rem small opening. Pull tight to cinch closed.

Arms (make 2)

With A, ch 3, join with sl st to form ring.

Rnd 1: Ch 1, sc 6 in ring, sl st in beg ch.

Inc rnd 2 Ch 1, 2 sc in each st around, sl st in first st of rnd—12 sc.

Rnd 3: Ch 1, sc in each st around, sl st in first st of rnd.

Switch to D.

Rnd 4: Ch 1, sc in each st around, sl st in first st of rnd.

Switch to E. From here through rem of arm, work 1 rnd with D and 1 rnd with E to make stripes.

Dec rnd 5: Ch 1, sc2tog, sc around, sl st in first st of rnd—11 sc.

Dec rnd 6: Ch 1, sc2tog, sc around, sl st in first st of rnd—10 sc.

Dec rnd 7: Ch 1, sc2tog, sc around, sl st in first st of rnd—9 sc.

Dec rnd 8: Ch 1, sc2tog, sc around, sl st in first st of rnd—8 sc.

Rnd 9 (arm cap): Ch 1, [sl st in next st] twice, sc in next st, [dc in next st] twice, sc in next st, [sl st in next st] twice, sl st in first st of rnd.

Fasten off.

Legs (make 2)

With G, ch 3, join with sl st to form ring.

Dec rnd 13: Ch 1, *sc2tog, sc in next 3 sts; rep from * around, sl st in first st of rnd—24 sc.

Dec rnd 14: Ch 1, *sc2tog, sc in next 2 sts; rep from * around, sl st in first st of rnd—18 sc.

Dec rnd 15: Ch 1, *sc2tog, sc in next st; rep from * around, sl st in first st of rnd—12 sc.

Stuff with polyfill.

Inc rnd 16: Ch 1, *2 sc in first st, sc in next 2 sts; rep from * around, sl st in first st of rnd—16 sc.

Body

Switch to D.

Inc rnd 17: Ch 1, *2 sc in first st, sc in next 3 sts; rep from * around, sl st in first st of rnd—20 sc.

Switch to E. From here through rnd 22, work 1 rnd with D and 1 rnd with E to make stripes.

Inc rnd 18: Ch 1, *2 sc in first st, sc in next 4 sts; rep from * around, sl st in first st of rnd—24 sc.

Rnds 19–22: Ch 1, sc in each st around, sl st in first st of rnd.

Switch to F.

Rnd 1: Ch 1, sc 6 in ring, sl st in beg ch.

Inc rnd 2 Ch 1, 2 sc in each st around, sl st in first st of rnd—12 sc.

Rnd 3: Ch 1, sc in each st around, sl st in first st of rnd.

Switch to F.

Rnds 4 and 5: Ch 1, sc in each st around, sl st in first st of rnd.

Fasten off.

Crown

With I and smaller hook, ch 21, join with sl st to form ring.

Rnd 1: Ch 1, sc in first ch and in each ch around—20 sc.

Rnd 2: Ch 1, sc in first st, *ch 1, sc in next 2 sts; rep from * until 1 st rem, ch 2, sc in last space. Fasten off.

Finishing Prince

Stuff Arms and Legs with small amounts of polyfil. Stuff yarn ends into limbs instead of cutting or weaving in, to help fill in limbs and use less stuffing. Leave about top third of arms unstuffed so they lie closer to body. Sew Arms to either side of Body with tall side of Arm Cap at top next to neck. Sew Legs to Body; do not pinch opening closed—sew around edge keeping circular shape intact.

Hair

Cut long strand of H. Using photo as guide, sew hair onto top of head with long stitches. Start at bottom back of head and work way up, eventually making long stitches across top of head to form side part. Sew crown to top of head.

TOWER

Platform

Note This is the piece that Rapunzel is standing on inside the Tower.

With L and larger hook, ch 3, join with sl st to form ring.

Rnd 1: Ch 1, 6 sc in ring, sl st in beg ch.

Inc rnd 2: Ch 1, 2 sc in each st around, sl st in first st of rnd—12 sc.

Inc rnd 3: Ch 1, *2 sc in first st, sc in next st; rep from * around, sl st in first st of rnd—18 sc.

Fasten off.

Bottom Base

Note Do not cut L and M for color change. Carry unused color up.

Ch 3, join with sl st to form ring.

Rnd 1: Ch 1, 6 sc in ring, sl st in beg ch.

Inc rnd 2: Ch 1, 2 sc in each st around, sl st in first st of rnd—12 sc.

Inc rnd 3: Ch 1, *2 sc in first st, sc in next st; rep from * around, sl st in first st of rnd—18 sc.

Inc rnd 4 Ch 1, *2 sc in first st, sc in next 2 sts; rep from * around, sl st in first st of rnd—24 sc.

Rnd 5: Ch 1, working in back loop of sts only, hdc in each st around, sl st in first st of rnd.

Rnd 6: With M, ch 1, hdc in each st around, sl st in first st of rnd.

Rnd 7: With L, *hdc in next 3 sts, dc in rnd below; rep from * around, sl st in first st of rnd.

Rep rnds 6 and 7 for 3 times more.

Dec rnd 14: With M, ch 1, *hdc2tog, hdc in next 2 sts; rep from * around, sl st in first st of rnd—18 hdc.

Rnd 15: With L, *hdc in next 2 sts, dc in rnd below; rep from * around, sl st in first st of rnd.

Sew upper level to inside of tower just below this rnd, stuff base of tower as you sew.

Rnd 16: With M, ch 1, hdc in each st around, sl st in first st of rnd.

Rnd 17: With L, *hdc in next 2 sts, dc in rnd below; rep from * around, sl st in first st of rnd.

Window Opening

Find center front of tower on previous rnd and mark center stitch. With RS facing, join L.

Row 1: Ch 1, sc in next 13 sts, sk over sl st and ch 1 at end/beg of previous rnd—13 sc.

5 sts at front of tower rem unworked for window opening.

Rows 2–5: Ch 1, turn, sc in next 13 sts.

At end of row 5, do not turn. Ch 5, hdc in st across window opening to rejoin in the rnd. Work around to this same point, putting one hdc st in each of the chs in front. At end of round, hdc in next 7 sts.

Fasten off.

Top

With M, ch 3, join with sl st to form ring.

Rnd 1: Ch 1, sc 6 in ring, sl st in beg ch.

Rnd 2: Ch 1, sc in each st around, sl st in first st of rnd.

Inc rnd 3: Ch 1, 2 sc in each st around, sl st in first st of rnd—12 sc.

Rnd 4: Ch 1, sc in each st around, sl st in first st of rnd.

Inc rnd 5: Ch 1, *2 sc in first st, sc in next st; rep from * around, sl st in first st of rnd—18 sc.

Rnd 6: Ch 1, sc in each st around, sl st in first st of rnd.

Inc rnd 7: Ch 1, *2 sc in first st, sc in next 2 sts; rep from * around, sl st in first st of rnd—24 sc.

Fasten off.

Sew Top to Tower using photo on page 67 as guide.

Appomattox Regional Library System
Hopewell, Virginia 23860
07/16